iPhone 15

Guide

An Illustrated Step By Step Manual For Seniors

Maddison Foster

Contents

 Apple Store App

 Clock App

 Apple TV App

 Maps App

 Books App

 Notes App

WED 28 Calendar App

 Files App

 Camera App

 iTunes App

 Calculator App

 News App

 Weather App

 Messages App

 Wallet App

 Stocks App

 Audio Recorder App

 Music App

 My iPhone App

 Photos App

 Mail App

 Video Call App

 Translate App

 Health App

 Contacts
App

 Podcasts
App

 Reminder
App

 Settings
App

 Compass
App

 Phone
App

 Tips
App

 Safari
App

| WI-FI |  | **LTE**
You are currently connected to your carrier's LTE network. This allows access to internet and other online services. | LTE |

CELL SIGNAL · · · · · 4G · · · · · 4G

DUAL CELL SIGNALS · · · · · 3G · · · · · 3G

AIRPLANE MODE · ✈ · · · · SOS · · · · SOS · · · ·

5G · 5G · **EMERGENCY SOS SATELITE** · 📡

5G UC
Your carrier's 5G network is available, and supported models can connect to the internet over that network. · 5G^{UC} · **WIFI CALLING** · Wi-Fi

5G+
Your carrier's 5G+ network is available, which can include your carrier's higher frequency version of 5G · 5G+ · **PERSONAL HOTSPOT** · ∞

VPN

SYNCING

NAVIGATION

NETWORK ACTIVITY

PHONE CALL

CALL FORWARDING

FACETIME

LOCK

SCREEN RECORDING

DO NOT DISTURB

CAMERA IN USE

PORTRAIT ORIENTATION LOCK

MICROPHONE IN USE

LOCATION SERVICES

ALARM

TTY
Communicate by telephone using Tele-
type (TTY) or real-time text (RTT) if
you have hearing or speech difficulties.

HEADPHONES
CONNECTED

CARPLAY

BATTERY

SIRI EYES FREE

BATTERY
CHARGING

EDGE

BLUETOOTH
BATTERY

AIRPLAY

VOICE CONTROL

SETTING UP YOUR iPHONE

Let's begin by turning on your iPhone and getting started. You can easily set up your new phone by following a few simple steps

CHARGING YOUR IPHONE

Your iPhone has an internal lithium-ion rechargeable battery, currently offering optimal performance. Your new iPhone can charge quicker, last longer, and is designed with extended battery life.

CHARGING INFORMATION

A battery icon with a lightning bolt shows the battery is charging. The battery icon in the top-right corner indicates the battery level or charging status. During synchronization or active use, charging may take a bit longer.

LOW BATTERY

If your iPhone's battery is running low, it may show a depleted battery icon, indicating that it needs at least 10 minutes of charging before you can use it again. If the battery is extremely low, the screen may be black for up to 2 minutes before the low-battery icon appears.

CHARGING METHODS

To charge your iPhone, you can choose from the following options:

1. Connect your iPhone to a power outlet using the provided charging cable, an Apple USB power adapter, or a compatible power adapter (available separately). For additional details, refer to "Power adapters for iPhone."

2. Place your iPhone face up on a MagSafe Charger or MagSafe Duo Charger connected to an Apple 20W USB-C or another compatible power adapter. Alternatively, you can use a Qi-certified charger. (These items are available separately.)

3. Connect your iPhone to your computer using a cable. Ensure your computer is powered on, as connecting to a powered-off computer may result in battery drainage instead of charging. Look for the charging icon ⚡ on the battery icon to confirm that your iPhone is charging.

If you think there may be liquid in your iPhone's charging port, do not plug in the charging cable.

OPTIMIZING IPHONE BATTERY CHARGING

Your iPhone offers a feature that helps reduce the rate of battery aging by limiting the time it remains fully charged. This setting utilizes machine learning to discern your daily charging routine, postponing charging beyond 80% until needed.

1. Open Settings ⚙ > Battery > Battery Health & Charging.
2. Depending on your iPhone model:
   - For iPhone 14 and earlier models: Activate "Optimized Battery Charging."
   - For iPhone 15 models: Select "Charging Optimization" and opt for "Optimized Battery Charging."

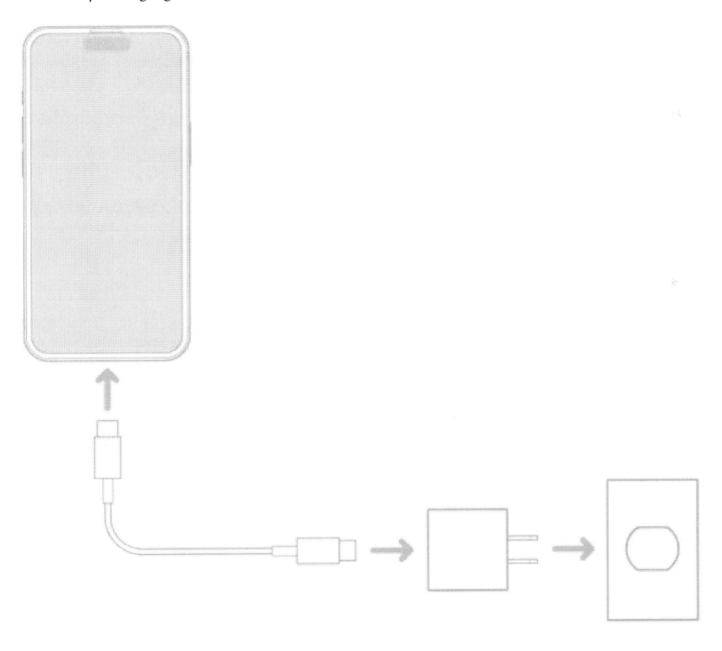

TURN ON YOUR IPHONE

To power on your iPhone, press and hold the side button situated on the right-hand side of your device.
This button also serves to wake your iPhone with a single press or to lock the screen after use.

If your phone fails to turn on, it may be due to a low battery. Simply connect it to a power source and allow it to charge. In case it still doesn't power on, you can seek help from Apple Support using another phone or visit the nearest Apple Store for assistance.

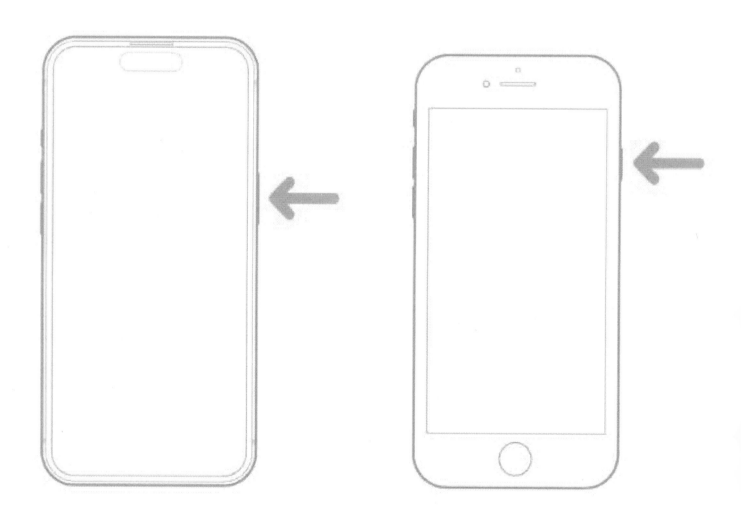

SETUP BASICS

Before we start setting up your iPhone, let's ensure you have everything you need:

INTERNET CONNECTION

Make sure you have an internet connection. If you're using Wi-Fi, you'll need the network name (Network ID) and password (Network Key). Look for the Wi-Fi symbol 📶 in the top right corner of your screen to confirm the connection.

CELLULAR SETUP

If you plan to use a cellular connection, insert your SIM card before setting up the iPhone.

APPLE ID

You can log in with your Apple ID, or create one during setup.

PAYMENT METHOD (OPTIONAL)

If you'd like to use the App Store or Apple Pay, have your debit or credit card handy to set up a payment method.

SWITCHING FROM ANDROID

If you're switching from an Android device, keep it nearby during the setup process.

ANDROID TO IPHONE

For Android users, you can download the 'Move to iOS' app from the Google Play Store. If you're not switching from an Android device, you can skip the last two steps."

MANUAL SETUP

Once you make sure that you have all the items ready, we can move on to setting up your iPhone. Here's a step-by-step guide to your iPhone for a manual setup.

SETTING LANGUAGE & REGION

Once you switch on your iPhone, you will be asked to choose your preferred language and region. All you have to do is tap on your desired language and region from the options shown on the screen. This will customize your iPhone settings to your liking and needs.

"QUICK START" OR "SET UP MANUALLY"

PREVIOUS USERS OF AN IPHONE BEFORE-

QUICK START

If you are an iPhone user, unlock your old device and bring it close to your new iPhone. A screen will appear on your old device with instructions to complete the "Quick Start" setup.

FIRST-TIME USERS OF IOS DEVICES OR IPHONES

- SET UP MANUALLY

If you're new to using an iOS device or iPhone, simply tap "Set Up Manually" on your screen to get started. Follow the on-screen instructions to set up your iPhone step-by-step, without needing an old iPhone. It's a simple and straightforward way to get your iPhone up and running

CONNECTING TO THE INTERNET

SELECT A WI-FI NETWORK

Choose a Wi-Fi network from the list of available networks. You'll need to enter your Wi-Fi password (Network Key) for the iPhone to connect to the network.

CONFIRM CONNECTION

After entering the password, keep an eye out for the Wi-Fi symbol (🛜) in the top right corner of your iPhone's screen. When you see this symbol, it means your iPhone is successfully connected to the internet via Wi-Fi.

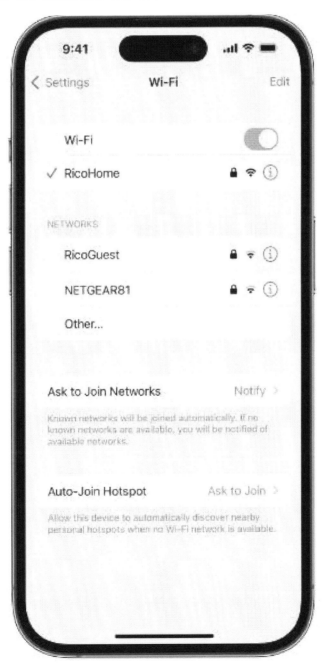

SECURITY ON YOUR IPHONE

SETTING UP FACE ID AND PASSCODE:

FACE ID (STEP 1)

You can use your face to set up Face ID for unlocking your iPhone. Just tap "Continue" and follow the instructions to scan your face for a successful setup.

PASSCODE (STEP 2)

In the second step, you'll create a passcode to secure your iPhone. You can choose either a 6-digit or a 4-digit unique number as your passcode. Make sure to remember this passcode because it's used to unlock your iPhone.

Note: Face ID is also used for secure transactions on the App Store and Apple Pay. If you prefer not to set up any security at this time, you can tap "Set up later" on both screens. However, it's generally recommended to have some form of security for your device.

"RESTORE" OR "TRANSFER DATA"

FOR THOSE WHO'VE USED IOS OR AN IPHONE BEFORE

- If you're upgrading from an older device, you can transfer your data to your new iPhone. Simply follow the on-screen options which include restoring from iCloud, transferring from a PC, Mac, or Android.

FOR FIRST-TIME IOS AND IPHONE USERS

- Tap "Don't Transfer Apps & Data" to proceed to the next step. This option is suitable if you're starting fresh without any previous data to transfer.

9:41

Transfer Your Apps & Data

Get your existing apps and information, like photos, notes and reminders, onto your new device.

☁ From iCloud Backup >

▢ From Another iPhone >

▭ From Mac or PC >

▢ From Android >

▢ Don't Transfer Anything >

CREATING OR SIGNING IN WITH APPLE ID

To continue, you'll need to sign in with your existing Apple ID. Please provide your Apple ID and password to sign in.

For those who don't have an Apple I

CREATE AN APPLE ID

If you don't have an Apple ID, tap "forgot the password or don't have an Apple ID." On the next screen, select "Create a Free Apple ID."

PROVIDE INFORMATION

You'll be asked for some basic information, including your name, birthday, and email address. If you've used an existing email for sign-up, you may receive a prompt to verify your email. Just follow the on-screen instructions to complete the verification.

NO EMAIL ADDRESS

If you don't have an email address, tap "Get a free iCloud email address" to generate a new Apple ID. This will provide you with a new email address associated with your Apple ID.

UPDATES & OTHER FEATURES

Here, you can set up auto-updates, Siri (a virtual voice assistant), and screentime.

AUTO-UPDATES: If you want your iPhone to automatically update itself, just tap "Continue." Your iPhone will take care of updates for you.

SETTING UP SIRI: To set up Siri, your helpful voice assistant, tap "Continue." Follow the on-screen instructions to enable Siri. Siri can assist you with calls, texts, device updates, weather, and more.

SCREEN TIME: If you'd like insights into how you use your phone, tap "Continue" to set up the "Screen Time" feature. It can provide useful information about your phone usage.

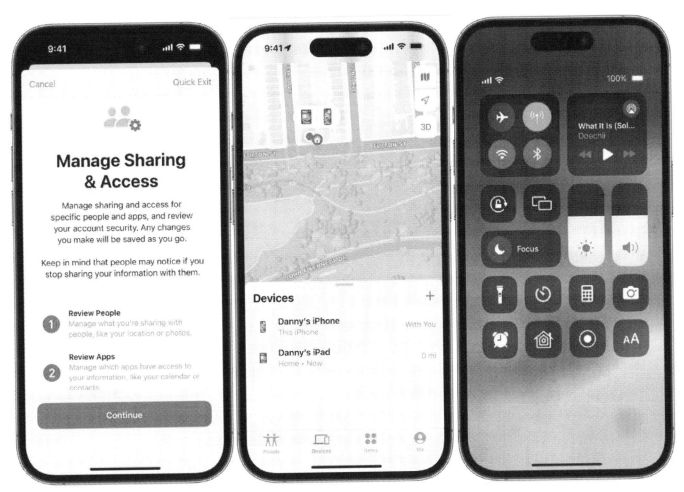

YOUR SETUP IS COMPLETE

Welcome to your new iPhone! Your setup is complete now. You can begin using your phone to connect to your loved ones, take pictures of your precious life moments and anything in between.

ESSENTIAL IPHONE FUNCTIONS

BUTTONS AND GESTURES

Discover how to interact with your iPhone effectively.
Explore fundamental gestures and buttons to assist you with everyday tasks.

BUTTONS & CAMERAS ON YOUR IPHONE

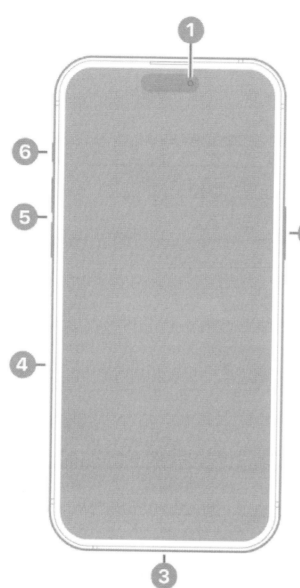

1. Front Facing Camera for selfies and videos.

2. A side button for Sleep/Wake function. You can also use it to turn your phone on and off.

3. SIM tray - Use it insert a physical SIM card to set up cellular connection.
A lighting cable connector which is used to charge your phone or connect it to your computer or other devices via lightning cable.

4. Volume buttons to adjust the ringtone volume or media volume on your iPhone.

5. Ring/Silent mode with lets you put your phone insolent mode or ing mode without having to unlock it first.

6. Action button gives you easy access to upto 8 different actions of apps. This will be explored in the next few pages.

Front Facing Camera for selfies and videos.

A side button for Sleep/Wake function. You can also use it to turn your phone on and off.

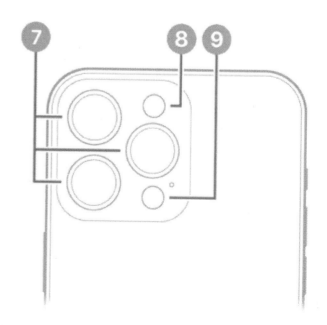

CHARGING PORT & OTHER FEATURES ON YOUR IPHONE

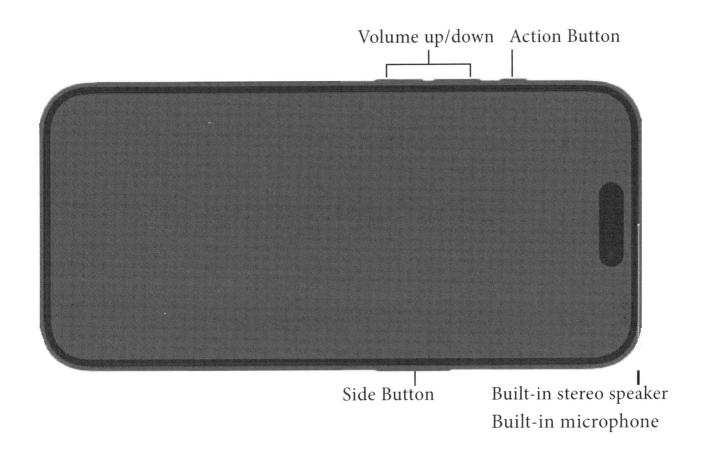

Volume up/down   Action Button

Side Button   Built-in stereo speaker
Built-in microphone

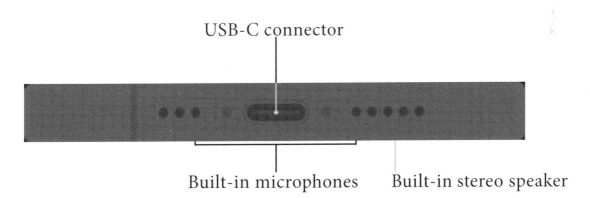

USB-C connector

Built-in microphones   Built-in stereo speaker

IPHONE 15, 15 PRO & 15 PRO MAX CAMERA

Depending on which iPhone you purchase, you will have either 2 phsycial lenses(iPhone 15) or 3 phsycial Lenes(15 Pro & 15 Pro Max).

IPHONE 15

The latest iPhone version, iPhone 15, boasts of a main camera that captures photos in super-high resolution, making it effortless to take remarkable pictures with intricate detail. Whether you're taking quick snapshots or capturing breathtaking landscapes, the results are nothing short of stunning.

The new camera features include:

Up to 4x resolution for capturing incredible levels of detail.

2x Telephoto lens, which effectively provides the functionality of a third camera, expanding your photography options.

IPHONE 15 PRO & PRO MAX

These models have all the features of the iphone 15 plus more!

The latest improvements in photography on iPhones are particularly noticeable in portrait shots. The best part is that you no longer have to switch to Portrait mode. Whenever you take a picture of a person, dog, or cat, the iPhone automatically captures depth information. This means you can view your photo instantly with an artistic blur effect, as if you took it in Portrait mode. Additionally, you can apply this effect later in the Photos app.

When it comes to the focal length of the Main camera (measured in millimeters, mm), you now have the freedom to choose your preferred lens. You can select from 24 mm, 28 mm, or 35 mm without the need for additional camera equipment. This versatility is possible through computational photography, which helps you adapt to different shooting situations with ease.

ACTION BUTTON

Learn how to customize the Action button on your iPhone 15 Pro or iPhone 15 Pro Max. This versatile button replaces the Ring/Silent switch and can be tailored to suit your needs. You can assign specific actions to it based on your preferences, making it perfect for frequently performed tasks.

1. 1. Go to "Settings  Action Button" on your device to access the Action Button Settings.

2. In the menu, you'll see icons representing various actions that can be assigned to the Action button. Swipe to the action you wish to use, and its name will appear below the selection dots. To enable Silent mode, swipe to the Bell Slash button. To choose another action, simply swipe to it.

3. If the selected action offers additional options, a Menu button will be visible below it. Tap this button to reveal a list of available options.

4. When customizing Shortcuts and Accessibility actions, you need to tap the blue button below the action and then select a specific option. Without this selection, the Action button won't perform any action.

Bell Slash button: Activate or deactivate Silent mode.

Do Not Disturb button: Enable or disable a specific Focus.

Voice Memo button: Start or stop recording a voice memo.

Flashlight button: Toggle the flashlight on or off.

Magnifier button: Access the Magnifier app.

Shortcut button: Open an app or execute your preferred shortcut.

Accessibility button: Swiftly access your preferred accessibility feature.

Camera button: Quickly open the Camera app for various photography options.

BASIC GESTURES

Navigating your iPhone is made easy with specific hand movements that execute a range of actions. These intuitive gestures include opening and closing apps, switching between them, accessing Siri, and utilizing Apple Pay. They are as simple as pressing physical buttons and swiping your fingers. To help you navigate your iPhone effortlessly, here is a compilation of uncomplicated and fundamental gestures.

Touch any icon on the screen with one finger. You can tap an App's icon to open it or enable or disable any feature.

The touch and hold gesture is used to reveal more options for apps or actions in the control center. Tap and hold the item until more options appear on your screen.

A swipe is a quick finger move across the screen. You can swipe from top to bottom or from left to right to scroll, move, or open another screen. For more functions, see the advanced gestures list below.

To scroll through the list of items like settings, webpages, or photos, swipe your finger from the top to bottom or from the bottom to the top without lifting it off the screen.

Bring your two fingers together and place them on the screen. Move them apart from each other while keeping them on screen. It will zoom in the picture or a webpage in the browser. Move the fingers towards each other to zoom out of the photo or webpage.

Here are some additional gestures that come in handy for an iPhone user.

SWIPE – Swipe up from the bottom edge of the screen. It will take you from a lock screen to your home screen where you can access apps and other features.

Use the same swipe gesture to close the already opened apps.

APP SWITCHER – Swipe up your finger from bottom to the center of the screen and then lift your finger. This will open the app switcher. Use it to access all the recently opened apps. Swipe through these apps from left to right and then tap the one you want to open.

If you wish to close an app, access the app switcher, tap and hold the app you wish to close, then swipe toward the top of the screen.

CONTROL CENTER – To access the "Control Center," swipe down with one finger from the top-right corner of the phone. Here you can access quick action controls of your iPhone. Touch and hold any icon to bring out more options.

To customize your control center go to Settings 🌐 > Control Center > Customize Control center

SWITCH BETWEEN APPS – You can switch between your opened apps by swiping from left to right or right to left on the bottom of your screen. You can only switch between the apps that are already opened in the background.

ACCESS "SIRI" – For "Siri," press and hold the power button & wait for Siri to appear and listen to your request. Siri listens as long as you are holding the button. It will complete your request once you release the button.

You can also set up "Hey Siri" to access Siri using your voice.

Go to Settings ⚙ > Siri & Search

APPLE PAY – If you have set up Apple Pay using your credit card, you can quickly access it by double-clicking the side button. Your phone will ask you to provide a Face ID to process the payments.

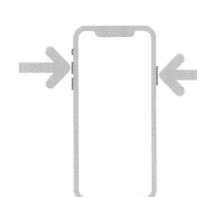

SCREENSHOT – Take a screenshot of your current screen by pressing the power button & volume up button and then quickly releasing them simultaneously.

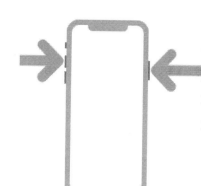

EMERGENCY SOS – In case of an SOS call, press and hold the power button along with any one of the volume buttons until the iPhone screen shows sliders. Swipe the SOS slider from left to right to make the call.

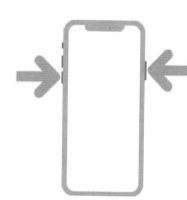

TURN OFF – Repeat the steps described for the SOS call in the previous step. Press & hold the side button and any of the volume buttons until sliders on the screen appear. This time, drag the power slider from left to right to turn off the iPhone.

You can also shut down your iPhone by going to Settings > General > Shut Down

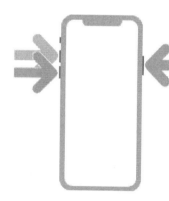

RESTART YOUR iPhone – If you need to force restart your phone for any reason, press & let go of the volume up button followed by doing the same for the volume down button (press & let go instantly), and lastly press & hold on the side button and wait for the Apple logo to appear on your screen before releasing the side button.

SETTINGS FOR YOUR APPLE ID AND ICLOUD

Your Apple ID is your gateway to various Apple services. It allows you to access apps and services while ensuring the security and storage of your private data through iCloud, a cloud storage platform. In this section, you'll gain comprehensive understanding about your Apple ID and iCloud services. This understanding will allow you to safeguard your data and maximize your iPhone's capabilities.

SIGNING IN AND CUSTOMIZING YOUR APPLE ID

You have the option to either create or sign in to your Apple ID during the initial iPhone setup or at a later time through the Settings. If you've initially set up your iPhone without an Apple ID, here's how you can create or sign in to your Apple ID through the Settings menu.

CREATING, SIGNING IN, OR RECOVERING YOUR APPLE ID

To create an Apple ID after the initial setup:

1. Open Settings ⚙️.
2. Tap "Sign in" at the top of the screen.
3. On the next screen, select "Don't have an Apple ID."
4. Then, tap "Create Free Apple ID."
5. Follow the on-screen instructions to create a new Apple ID for your iPhone.

If you've already created an Apple ID but didn't sign in during setup, you can sign in by following these steps:

1. Go to Settings ⚙️.
2. Tap "Sign in" at the top of the screen.
3. Enter your Apple ID and password.
4. Tap "Sign in."

If you've forgotten your Apple ID or password, you can recover your ID through Settings:

1. Navigate to Settings ⚙️.
2. Tap "Sign in" at the top of the screen.

These steps will help you create, sign in to, or recover your Apple ID, ensuring you have access to your iPhone's full range of features and services.

Note: Keep your Phone number and email that you used in Apple ID ready, as you'll use it to reset your password. You will receive some confirmation codes in order for Apple to confirm that it's you resetting your password.

CHANGE APPLE ID INFORMATION

Once you've logged in, you can easily modify or refresh your Apple ID details within the Apple ID settings. Here's how you can access and update your Apple ID information or settings on your iPhone:

1. Open Settings .
2. Tap on your Name displayed at the top of the settings screen.
3. On the next screen, you'll find various options related to your personal information. These include:

- Name, Phone Numbers, Email

- Password & Security

- Payment & Shipping

- Subscription

4. Select any of the above options to view your current information or make updates as needed.

In addition to managing your personal information, you can also oversee other aspects of your Apple ID and iCloud, such as iCloud storage, App store purchases, Find My, and family sharing, all within this section. These features are all interconnected with your Apple ID and iCloud account.

ICLOUD STORAGE & SERVICES

iCloud, offered by Apple, serves as your personal cloud storage solution with versatile applications. It securely stores various elements such as photos, documents, music, messages, notes, backups, and even your home screen preferences, making them accessible at any moment. Beyond storage, iCloud boasts a remarkable feature: it seamlessly synchronizes your data across all your iOS devices, including iPhone, iPad, MacBook, and iMac.

ICLOUD+

iCloud+ represents Apple's premium cloud subscription service, offering enhanced storage for your photos, files, and backups, along with exclusive features available solely to subscribers. There are three iCloud+ plans available:

iCloud+ with 50GB Storage:

- 50GB of storage
- iCloud Private Relay
- Hide My Email Address
- Custom Email Domain
- HomeKit Secure Video support for one camera
- Ability to share everything with up to five other family members.

iCloud+ with 200GB Storage:

- 200GB of storage
- iCloud Private Relay
- Hide My Email Address
- Custom Email Domain
- HomeKit Secure Video support for up to five cameras
- Ability to share everything with up to five other family members.

iCloud+ with 2TB Storage:

- 2TB of storage
- iCloud Private Relay
- Hide My Email Address
- Custom Email Domain
- HomeKit Secure Video support for an unlimited number of cameras
- Ability to share everything with up to five other family members.

Currently, this is the iCloud+ pricing from Apple:

- 50 GB for $0.99
- 200 GB for $2.99
- 2 TB for $9.99

ICLOUD+ SETTINGS

To access your iCloud+ settings:
1. Open Settings 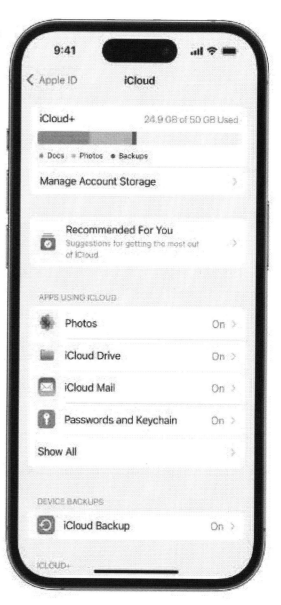.
2. Tap on your Name displayed at the top of the settings screen.
3. Select iCloud.

Within your iCloud settings, you can manage various features and information:

PHOTOS

Enabling this feature allows you to store your personal photos on iCloud, freeing up space on your iPhone. You can also disable it if you prefer not to store your data on iCloud.

ICLOUD BACKUP

This feature automatically backs up your personal apps and data to iCloud, ensuring you don't lose data even if your phone is lost.

KEYCHAIN

Use this to save and sync your passwords and login information across iOS devices.

PRIVATE BETA REPLAY (ONLY ON ICLOUD+)

This feature allows you to hide your IP address while using the internet for enhanced privacy.

HIDE MY EMAIL

This feature conceals your email address from potential scammers and marketing campaigns, enhancing your online security and privacy.

To save and sync your other data across all your IOS devices, enable all the following features in your iCloud or iCloud+ settings list:

- iCloud Drive
- Contacts
- Calenders
- Reminders
- Notes
- Messages
- Safari
- Stocks
- Home
- Health
- Wallet
- Game center
- Siri
- Books
- Shortcuts
- Weather

iCloud also stores app data from apps other than default apps on Apple. All the apps that support the iCloud feature will appear in the list under the iCloud settings. You can enable or disable backup or data sharing according to your preferences and use.

PERSONALIZATION

Customize Your iPhone to Suit Your Preferences

Discover how to personalize your iPhone by adjusting settings such as wallpaper, ringtones, date, time, and more to create a tailored experience that suits your style and needs.

CHANGING YOUR IPHONE WALLPAPER

Personalize your display background with a picture of your choice. The iPhone offers a diverse selection of images in the wallpaper gallery for you to browse. You can pick from three categories: dynamic, still, or live wallpapers. If none of these appeal to you, you can also set a favorite photo from your own gallery as your wallpaper.

WALLPAPER SETTINGS

To open wallpaper settings,
go to Settings 🌐 >
Wallpaper.

Tap "Choose a New Wallpaper" to access more options related to Wallpaper.

SELECTING A NEW

WALLPAPER

You can choose your new wallpaper from the

provided categories: Dynamic, Stills, or Live. Each category offers a variety of wallpapers for you to explore. Simply tap the wallpaper you like to set it as your new background.

USING YOUR PHOTO GALLERY IMAGES

Beneath these categories, you'll find your photo gallery albums. To set one of your pictures as your wallpaper:

1. Tap "All Photos" or select the specific "Album" containing the image you want.
2. Choose the desired picture to set as your wallpaper.

ADJUSTING WALLPAPER OPTIONS

Upon tapping the new wallpaper or picture, you'll be presented with some options on the next screen:

- Perspective Zoom: Some wallpapers support this feature, marked with a 🔘 symbol. Perspective Zoom changes the wallpaper angle as you move your iPhone, providing a more dynamic view.

- Dark Mode: Wallpapers with this symbol can shift from bright colors to darker tones.

After adjusting zoom and light or dark mode, tap "Set" in the bottom right corner. You'll then be asked whether you want the chosen wallpaper for your home screen, lock screen, or both. Simply select your desired option, and your wallpaper will be updated accordingly.

ADJUST COLOR & BRIGHTNESS TO YOUR PREFERENCES

The iPhone uses three modes to adjust the color and brightness according to your needs. These modes are Dark Mode, Night Shift, and True Tone. All three modes work differently. Your iPhone also adjusts brightness according to your surroundings once you enable the option from settings.

The following are your brightness and color options on your iPhone:

ADJUST BRIGHTNESS MANUALLY OR AUTOMATICALLY

For a manual adjustment of your screen brightness:

- Swipe your finger from the top-right corner towards the bottom to open the control center.
- Look for the brightness bar with the ☀ symbol.
- Drag it up or down to manually adjust the brightness of your screen.

To let your phone adjust the brightness automatically according to your surroundings:

- Go to Settings ⚙ > Tap "Accessibility"
- From the list showing on your screen, tap "Display & Text Size."
- Enable the "Auto-Brightness" feature.

DARK MODE

In Dark Mode, your phone changes the light colors to darker ones (everything that has a white background will now have a black background). It helps you use your phone in low light. With Dark Mode turned on, you can use your phone in the dark without the lighter colors being hard on your eyes.

You can turn Dark Mode on & off from the control center or by going into the Settings. You can even set it to change automatically depending on what time of the day it is.

DARK MODE IN CONTROL CENTER

- Open the control center and long press ☀ to show more options.
- Tap ◐ to turn the Dark Mode on or off.

TURN ON DARK MODE IN SETTINGS OR SCHEDULE IT

- Go to Settings ⚙ > Tap "Display & Brightness."
- At the top of the next screen, you can see the option of "Light Mode" or "Dark Mode."
- Tap any of the two to switch between the two modes.

To automatically turn Dark Mode on or off, enable the "Automatic" feature just below the light & dark mode option, then follow the instructions below to schedule it.

- After you enable "Automatic," tap the "Options" that will appear below the toggle button.
- Choose "Sunset to Sunrise" to let the iPhone switch the modes depending on the sunset and sunrise time.
- To schedule the modes at your preferred times, tap "Custom Schedule."
- You'll see two options, light mode and dark mode, with a clock option in front of both the options.
- Enter the time for both modes to let your phone switch between modes at your given time.

NIGHT SHIFT

Night shift makes the screen light dimmer and less hard on your eyes, especially when you are using your phone in darker places. Here's how to turn it on, off, or schedule it to your needs.

- Open control center, long press ◐ to show more options on the screen.
- Tap "Night Shift" to turn it on or off.

To turn Night Shift on manually or to schedule it, you need to turn it on from settings.

In settings, it also gives you the option to adjust the tone of the night shift by sliding the adjustment slider between less warm or more warm options.

- Go to Settings ⚙ > tap "Display & Brightness"
- Tap "Night Shift" to reveal more options.
- Tap "Scheduled" to set the time to turn Night Shift on & off.
- Slide the adjustment slider to set the color that best suits your eyes.

TRUE TONE

True Tone gives your document, photo, or any content on your screen a more natural display using the true tone feature. Enabling True Tone will allow your iPhone to adjust the color and brightness of the content on the screen according to the external environment.

To turn True Tone on & off, follow the steps below:

- Go to Settings ⚙ > tap "Display & Brightness."
- Tap the "True Tone" toggle button to turn it on or off.

ORGANIZE YOUR IPHONE HOME SCREEN

Efficiently arrange your apps on the home screen for easy access and a tailored experience. You can move, delete, create folders, and add widgets to your home screen.

TO REARRANGE APPS

1. Tap and hold any app icon on the home screen until additional options appear.
2. Select "Edit Home Screen," and the icons will start to wiggle.
3. Tap and hold the app you want to move.
4. Drag it across the screen to change its position on the same page or drag it to the edge of the screen to move to the next page.
5. Release the icon to place it in the new location.
6. Tap "Done" at the top-right corner when you've finished organizing the apps.

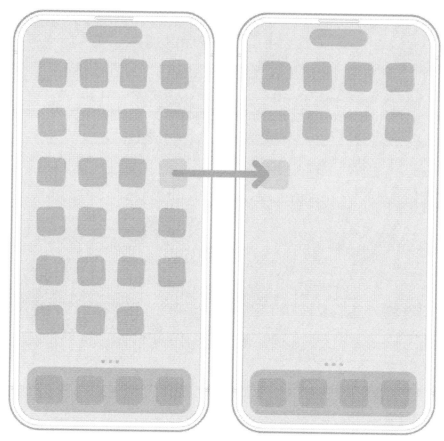

ADDING WIDGETS

Widgets are small, informative displays on your home screen that show app data without opening the app itself.

1. Tap and hold any app icon on the home screen to reveal more options.
2. Select "Edit Home Screen," and the icons will begin to shake.
3. Tap the ⊕ icon at the top-right corner of the screen.
4. You'll see a list of available widgets.
5. Choose a widget from your desired app and select a widget style.
6. Tap the desired widget to add it to your home screen. Adjust its position by dragging it.
7. Tap "Done" when you're satisfied.

Tap to add widgets to your Lock Screen.

ADJUSTING SOUND & VIBRATION ON YOUR IPHONE

Your iPhone offers various options for customizing sound and vibrations, including volume control and haptic feedback settings. Here's how to change and fine-tune these settings

ADJUSTING SOUND AND VIBRATION SETTINGS

1. Open Settings ⚙.
2. Tap "Sound & Haptics."

VOLUME CONTROL

- Drag the slider to adjust the volume for all notifications on your iPhone.

CHANGING RINGTONES

- To modify the ringtone for different types of notifications, tap the specific notification category (e.g., ringtone, text tone, voicemail, mail, calendars, reminders, airdrop).

- Scroll through the available ringtones, tap one to listen, and select your preferred tone as the new ringtone or notification sound.

CUSTOMIZING VIBRATION PATTERNS

- To change the vibration pattern, tap the notification type (e.g., ringtone, text tone, voicemail, mail, calendar, reminder, airdrop).

- Tap "Vibration" at the top of the ringtone list.

- Here, you can choose a different vibration pattern or create your own custom vibration pattern for a specific type of notification.

HAPTIC FEEDBACK

Haptic feedback provides tactile vibrations while performing certain tasks on your iPhone, such as long-pressing or refreshing social media feeds.

To enable or disable this feature:
1. Open the Settings app ⚙.

2. Tap "Sound & Haptics."

3. Toggle the "System Haptics" switch to turn haptic feedback on or off.

Note: The "Sound & Haptic" setting controls all vibrations on your iPhone. Disabling this feature will turn off vibrations for all notifications, including incoming calls and messages.

CHANGING DATE, TIME, REGION, LANGUAGE, AND DEVICE NAME

You have the flexibility to modify various aspects of your device information, including date & time, language & region, and even your device name.
Here's how you can make these adjustments:

DATE & TIME

1. 1. Go to Settings 🌐 > General > Date & Time.
2. 2. Enable "Set Automatically" for your iPhone to set the time based on your location.
   - If you prefer to set the time manually, disable the automatic option and input the desired time.
3. 3. Choose between displaying time in a 12-hour or 24-hour format by toggling the respective option.

REGION & LANGUAGE

1. Navigate to Settings 🌐 > General > Region & Language.
2. Make adjustments to your Region, Language, Calendar, and Temperature Units.
3. Preview how your iPhone will display region, language, and calendar information after applying the changes.

CHANGING DEVICE NAME

1. Go to Settings 🌐 > General > About > Name.
2. Clear the existing name and enter a new one of your choice.
3. Tap "Done" in the lower-right corner of the keyboard to save the new device name.

By following these steps, you can effectively customize your device information to better suit your preferences and needs.

APP STORE

Explore Your App Universe with One Simple Tap!

Uncover, Download, and Manage Apps, Services, and Subscriptions Effortlessly.

THE APP STORE YOUR ULTIMATE APP HAVEN

With the App Store, getting your favorite apps, games, fonts, and more is as easy as a single tap. Offering a vast selection of over two million apps, there's something for everyone. All you need is your Apple ID and an internet connection to dive into a world of digital possibilities.

TODAY

Apple regularly spotlights apps and in-app events, ensuring you stumble upon fresh and exciting options each day.

GAMES

Whether you're into online gaming, multiplayer adventures, action-packed races, or more, the App Store has a wide range of thrilling games to choose from.

APPS

Stay in the loop with the latest releases and top-rated apps that can enhance your digital experience. Explore top charts, new arrivals, or specific categories to find the perfect app for your needs.

ARCADE

For ad-free, premium gaming experiences, Apple Arcade offers a curated collection of games. A subscription is required, but it's worth it for a seamless gaming journey.

SEARCH

Want something specific? Simply use the search bar at the top to find apps by name or keywords. The App Store makes it effortless to locate exactly what you're looking for.

With the App Store's user-friendly interface and extensive catalog, discovering and enjoying new apps and experiences has never been more convenient.

HOW TO PURCHASE OR DOWNLOAD APPS FROM THE APP STORE

Open the App Store by tapping the and locate the app you want to download.

Tap on the app's name to access more details such as its size, rating, reviews, developer info, compatibility, and supported languages.

If the app is free, simply tap "Get" to initiate the download. For paid apps, you'll see the app's price instead of "Get." Just tap the price and confirm the purchase using Face ID or your Apple ID password to start the download.

Note: If you've already downloaded a free app or purchased it from the App Store, you'll see an icon in place of the price or "Get."

HOW TO UTILIZE APPLE GIFT CARDS IN THE APP STORE

Apple Gift Cards allow you to load money directly into your Apple ID account, which you can later use for app purchases or subscriptions on the App Store. You can obtain gift cards from the Apple website or your nearest Apple Store, and you can even send them as gifts to family and friends who are Apple users.

TO REDEEM OR SEND AN APPLE GIFT CARD

Go to the App Store and tap your "Profile Icon" located in the top-right corner of your screen.

On the following screen, tap either "Redeem Gift Card or Code" or "Send Gift Card By Email." Follow the on-screen instructions to redeem or send the gift card.

ADDING FUNDS TO YOUR APPLE ID

You can also add funds to your Apple ID, which can be used for purchasing apps, games, subscriptions, or making in-app purchases. Similar to using a debit/credit card or an Apple Gift Card, these funds are added to your balance, which you can then utilize on the App Store.

To Add Funds to Your Apple ID, ensure you've added a payment method, such as your debit or credit card, to your Apple ID. Here's how to do it:

1. Go to the App Store and tap your "Profile Icon" in the top-right corner of your screen.

2. Tap "Add Funds To Apple ID."

3. Choose an amount displayed on your screen or select "Other" to enter your desired amount.

4. Tap "Next" and confirm your purchase using Face ID or your password. This will add the funds to your Apple ID balance."

MANAGEMENT OF SUBSCRIPTIONS, DOWNLOADS, AND PURCHASES IN THE APP STORE

The App Store settings provide a convenient hub for overseeing and adjusting your subscriptions, downloads, and purchases, all from one location. You can even tailor your App Store experience to display only the apps and features that interest you

To view all your purchased apps:

1. Go to the App Store and tap your "Profile Icon" in the top-right corner of your screen.
2. Tap "Purchased."
3. On the next screen, you'll find two categories: "All," where you can view all your downloaded and purchases made with your Apple ID, and "Not on this iPhone," which displays purchases made with your Apple ID on other devices but not yet downloaded onto your iPhone.

MANAGE YOUR SUBSCRIPTIONS WITH APPLE ID

4. Go to the App Store and tap your "Profile Icon" in the top-right corner of your screen.
5. Tap "Subscriptions." You may be asked to sign in again.
6. Here, you can view all your subscriptions and choose to renew or cancel any subscriptions made in the App Store.

CUSTOMIZING AND RESTRICTING YOUR APP STORE

You have the ability to customize how your App Store operates. To access and adjust the App Store settings, follow these steps:

Go to Settings and tap "App Store"

AUTOMATIC DOWNLOADS:

Enable "Apps" to allow your iPhone to download apps and purchases made on your other iOS devices. Turn on "App Updates" to have your phone automatically download and install new updates.

MOBILE DATA

Use caution with "Automatic Downloads" on cellular connections, as it may consume your monthly data. Consider keeping it off and download/update apps when connected to Wi-Fi. You can also specify if you want your phone to download larger apps using cellular data.

VIDEO AUTOPLAY

Select between "On," "Off," or "Wi-Fi Only" options. This determines if the App Store will play preview videos while downloading.

IN-APP RATINGS & REVIEWS

Toggle this option on if you want to review your favorite apps.

Offload Unused Apps: Enabling this feature will remove unused apps after a period while retaining the data. You'll still see the app's icon on your home screen. If you want to re-download it, simply tap the icon, and the iPhone will fetch the app if it's still available on the App Store. Turn this feature on to save storage space on your iPhone.

Take control of your App Store experience by customizing these settings to suit your preferences and needs.

APPS ON YOUR IPHONE

Enjoy Apple's pre-installed apps and in-app functionalities for entertainment, seamless connections, and enhanced productivity.

App Store

BOOKS

Enjoy the convenience of buying and enjoying your favorite books, whether you prefer reading or listening while on the move. With "Books," you can also easily view, print, or annotate PDFs. Here's how to purchase your books or audiobooks:

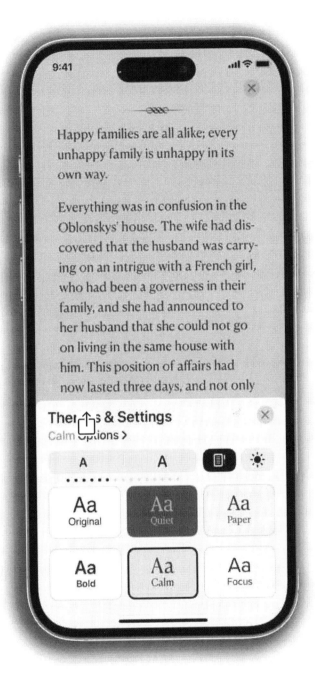

1. Open Books 📖 and choose "Book Store" or "Audiobooks" to explore the available titles in both stores.
2. Select any title to preview it or listen to a sample on the Audiobook store.
3. Click "Buy" to proceed with the purchase, or tap "Get" if the book is free to download.
4. Access your purchased books and audiobooks in the "Library," where you can read, listen, and organize your collection.

To seamlessly handle PDFs in the Books app:

1. To open and read a PDF, simply open the PDF file, tap   , and select "Books."

2. For sharing or printing your PDF:

   • Open the PDF file, tap 📤 , and access the share sheet. Choose the apps you wish to share the PDF with.

   • To print the PDF, tap "Print" from the share sheet, and then select from the available printers to complete the printing process.

CALCULATOR

The Calculator app is a versatile tool that handles all the fundamental functions you'd expect from a standard calculator. It's capable of performing a wide range of calculations, spanning from basic arithmetic operations to more advanced trigonometric, exponential, and logarithmic calculations.

To access the Calculator app, tap the "Calculator"  icon on your home screen or open the control center and select the "calculator icon."

For standard arithmetic functions, simply use the calculator while holding your phone upright in portrait orientation.

To change the standard calculator into scientific mode, simply rotate your iPhone sideways (landscape orientation).

ADDITIONAL FUNCTIONS ON THE CALCULATOR

Unlock the Calculator's Hidden Features:

1. Copy & Paste Results: Want to save your calculation results? Tap and hold the current result on the screen, then select "Copy" to store the result on your clipboard. Now, you can paste it into other apps like messages or notes by tapping and holding the cursor and choosing "Paste."

2. Quick Error Correction: Made a mistake while typing numbers? No worries. Just swipe right or left while keeping your finger on the numbers, and the calculator will remove one digit at a time for precise error correction.

3. Clear Your Calculations: To clear the last calculation, tap "C." If you need a fresh start and want to erase all previous calculations, simply tap "AC" to reset the calculator.

CALENDAR

Your iPhone's calendar is your trusty companion for keeping track of appointments, meetings, invitations, and more. Here are some essential tips for navigating the Calendar app:

1. Customize Your View: Tailor your calendar view to your preference. Simply zoom in or out in calendar apps to change your perspective. In week and month views, you can also find ▣ at the top of the screen, which allows you to switch between different calendar appearances.

2. Multiple Calendars: The Calendar app supports multiple calendars simultaneously. To add or remove additional calendars, follow these steps:

   • Go to Settings ⚙ and tap "Calendar."

   • Select "Alternative Calenda

   • Choose from the available

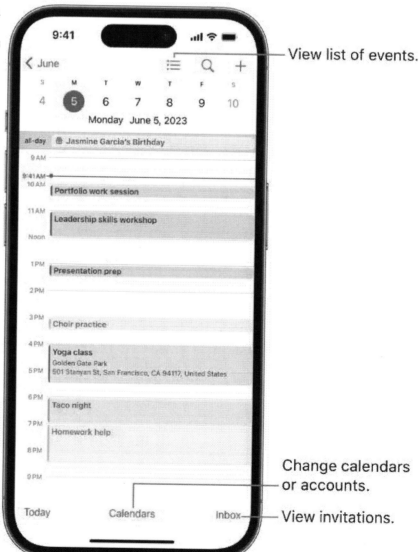

View list of events.

Change calendars or accounts.

View invitations.

3. Adding Events with Alerts Never miss an important event by adding events with alerts:

52

- Open "Calendar" $\overset{\text{WED}}{28}$ and access the "day view."

- Tap ✛ at the top-right corner.

- Fill in event details, including start and end times, repeats, or travel time.

- Set an alert for the event by tapping "Alert" and choosing the desired notification time.

4. Attachments: Attach photos or files to your calendar events:

   - Tap "Add Attachment," select the file you want to attach, and then tap "Done."

5. Sharing Events: Share your events with others, whether they are family members, friends, or colleagues:

   - Go to "Calendar" $\overset{\text{WED}}{28}$ and open the event you want to share or create a new one.

   - Tap "Invitees" and add the people you want to invite to your event.

6. Editing Events: Easily make changes to your existing events:

   - Go to "Calendar" $\overset{\text{WED}}{28}$ and find the event.

   - Tap "Edit" at the top-right corner to update event details.

7. Deleting Events: If you need to remove an event from your calendar:

   - Go to "Calendar" $\overset{\text{WED}}{28}$ and locate the event.

   - Tap "Edit" at the top-right corner, then scroll down and tap "Delete Event."

8. Using Calendars with iCloud: iCloud ensures that your events stay synchronized across all your iOS devices. Here's how to set it up:

   - Go to Settings ⚙ and tap "Your Name" at the top of your screen.

   - Select "iCloud" and enable "Calendar" to sync your events across all your iOS devices.

Enjoy the convenience and organization that your iPhone's calendar offers, and keep your events secure and up-to-date with iCloud.

CAMERA

To open the Camera app, simply tap the Camera icon on your iPhone Home Screen, swipe left on your iPhone Lock Screen, or long-press the Camera button on the Lock Screen. You can even use Siri by saying "Open Camera" to launch the app.

When the Camera is active, a green dot appears in the top-right corner of the screen to ensure your privacy and security.

ACCESSING THE CAMERA

On the iPhone 15, you can customize the Action button to open the Camera or press on the app on your home screen.

UNDERSTANDING BASIC CONTROLS AND MODES

To take a photo, simply open the Camera app  tap the Shutter button or press either volume button to capture the shot.

You can also switch between different modes by swiping left or right on the camera screen. The available modes include Video, Time-lapse, Slo-mo, Pano, Portrait, Cinematic, and Square. On iPhone 11 and later, you can tap the Camera Controls button and select 4:3, Square, or 16:9 aspect ratios.

Following are features of every mode:

Photo – This mode simply take photos without any effects and opens up when you tap the camera icon.

Videos – It simply records a video without any specialized effects.

Slo-mo – Adds a slow-motion effect to your videos to make them more enjoyable.

Time-lapse – A video mode that speeds up your recorded video.

Pano – The captures panoramic scenes or when you need to capture a wider landscape.

Portrait – Capture professional photos by applying depth-of-field to your photos.

Cinematic – A portrait mode for your videos that applies depth-of-field to your videos.

54

Square – Capture photos in square ratio. You can also choose your desired ratio by taping at top of the screen, and then choosing from the given option i.e. 4:3, 16:9, and square.

To zoom in and out on your photos and videos, use the pinch gesture on the object. Alternatively, you can see the zoom buttons just above the modes. Tap the zoom between 0.5x – 4x range to zoom in and out. Tap and hold the toggles to zoom more precisely between the given range.

MANUAL FOCUS AND EXPOSURE ADJUSTMENT

- Open the Camera app 📷.
- Tap on the screen where you want to set the focus area. This will show you the automatic focus area and exposure settings.
- Next to the focus area, drag the ☀ button up or down to fine-tune the exposure to your liking.

If you want to lock your manual focus and exposure settings for multiple shots, tap and hold the focus area until you see "AE/AF Lock." To unlock the settings, just tap on the screen.

PRECISE EXPOSURE CONTROL

- Tap on the ⌃ button.
- Tap on the ± button, then use the slider to adjust the exposure precisely.
- The exposure settings will remain locked until you reopen the Camera app.

To save your exposure control preferences, go to Settings > Camera > Preserve Settings, and turn on "Exposure Adjustment."

FLASH CONTROL

- To manually control the flash, tap on the ⚡ button. You can turn it on or off as needed.
- For more control, tap on the ⌃ button, then tap on the ⚡ button below the frame

to choose between "Auto," "On," or "Off."

APPLY FILTERS

- Open the Camera app 📷 in Photo or Portrait mode.
- Tap on the ⌃ button, then tap on the ⊛ button.
- Swipe left or right to preview filters, and tap on one to apply it.

USE THE TIMER

- Tap on the ⌃ button in the Camera app 📷 .
- Tap on the 🕐 button, and choose either a 3-second or 10-second delay.
- Press the shutter button to start the timer, giving you time to get into the shot.

GRID AND LEVEL FOR COMPOSITION

- Go to Settings ⚙ > Camera, and turn on "Grid" and "Level."
- This will display a grid and level on the camera screen, helping you compose and straighten your shots.

STRAIGHTEN AND EDIT IN PHOTOS

- After taking a photo, you can further align and edit it in the Photos app 🌸 .
- Use editing tools to adjust the horizontal and vertical perspective, ensuring your photos look just the way you want them.

TAKE PORTRAIT PHOTOS & RECORD CINEMATIC VIDEOS

Portrait photos and cinematic videos create a beautiful effect by taking your personal photography to the next level. These modes create photos and videos with your desired object sharp, in focus, and with the background blurred to make your content more cinematic.

To take the best shot with portrait mode, open the camera app 📷 and choose "Portrait Mode." Portrait mode gives you a variety of effects to choose from.

Tap and drag the 🔶 to the left to choose the following option available in portrait mode photography:

- Natural Light: Captures photos in their natu

- Studio Light: Offers an additional color and sharpness in your photos making them brighter and more lit up.

- Contour Light: Most efficient to capture dramatic photos with high and low lights casting on objects.

- Stage Light: Your object such as your face or your pet is lit up against a deep black background. Stage light effect has a further two types including light-mono and high-key light mono that offers pictures in black and white effect or grayscale effects. Choose the one that makes your photo look best.

The light effects on portrait mode are adjustable. To set the lighting effects in portrait, tap ⌃ at the top of your camera screen and drag the slider to adjust the lighting effects for your photo.

Change the intensity of the portrait mode to only blur backgrounds as much as you need. You can even change the focus on captured photos:

- Choose the portrait mode in the camera app and bring the object in focus.

- Look for ◉ at the top-right corner and tap it. Use the slider to adjust the focus.

- Drag the focus-slider to increase or decrease the blur intensity of the background.

- Once the focus is all set, tap "Shutter" to take a portrait picture.

To change the focus on already captured photos, go to the Photos app 🏵 > Open the desired photo > Tap "Edit" > Tap "Portrait" to turn the effect on and off or adjust the focus on your captured photos.

The cinematic mode in the video offers a variety of options to help you record high-quality personal videos with professional effects.

To record a cinematic video on your iPhone:

- Open the Camera app 📷 and choose "Cinematic Mode."
- Turn your phone sideways in landscape orientation and then tap to reveal the following options

f — Just like the portrait mode in photos, you can adjust the focus on video by clicking focus and dragging the slider.

⚡ — Turn the flashlight on & off or select "Auto" to turn it on and off automatically depending on external light.

1× — Tap 1x button to switch between the telephoto and wide-angle to capture fewer or more objects in one frame.

⊕ — Control the exposure to your videos. Use the slider to make your videos dark or bright

- Once your frame is set for video, Tap ⚫ button to record the video. Tap it again to stop the recording.

VIEW YOUR PHOTOS & VIDEOS

All your photos and videos are saved in the Photo app ✻. You can view your recently taken photos and videos, directly from the camera app or Photo app.

To view your photos & videos directly from your camera app, tap the photo in the lower-left corner of the camera app. It will open your recently taken photos and videos on your iPhone. Swipe through the photos and videos to view your recently taken shots. Tap "All Photos" at the top right corner to view your photos in the Photo app.

CLOCK

The Clock app  on your iPhone is a versatile tool that goes beyond being a simple stopwatch, alarm, or timer. It also aids in productivity and sleep cycle tracking.

MANAGING ALARMS

Setting, modifying, or deleting alarms
1. Open the Clock app and tap "Alarm" at the bottom of your screen.
2. Tap the ┼ icon at the top-right to add a new alarm.
3. Configure the alarm time, alert, and frequency as needed.
4. Save the alarm.
5. You can easily toggle alarms on and off from the list.

To adjust the settings of existing alarms:

•   Tap "Edit" in the top left corner of the Clock > Alarm.

•   Select the alarm you wish to modify.

•   Make desired changes and tap "Save."

DELETING ALARMS

1. Tap "Edit" in the top left corner of the Clock > Alarm.
2. Tap the ⊖ button and then "Delete" to remove the alarm.
3. Tap "Done" when finished.

MONITOR YOUR SLEEP CYCLE

The Clock app offers a valuable feature for monitoring your sleep cycle, which can be managed through the Health app on your iPhone. It helps set your bedtime and wake time while tracking your device activity to gauge your actual sleep duration.

Access the Health app ♥ to configure your sleep cycle. Once set up, you can adjust wake-up and bedtime reminders.

After tapping "Change," your screen provides options. Drag the slider around the clock to set new wake-up and bedtime. Your wake-up time is indicated by the clock's outer circle, while bedtime is shown inside it. Adjusting these reveals your total sleep hours below the slider. In "Alarm Options," you can configure wake-up alarms, snooze, and "Sounds & Haptics."

WORLD CLOCK

Navigate to the Clock app  > "World Clock."

4. Tap the ➕ icon, then search or select cities to add.
5. Tap a city to include it in your world clock list.
6. Use "Edit" to rearrange or "Delete" to remove cities.

USE STOPWATCH

Record time for specific tasks by opening the stopwatch and tapping "Start." If you need to track multiple intervals, press the "Lap" button, and laps will appear below. To stop, tap "Stop," and reset with "Reset."

SET TIMER

Configure a countdown timer by tapping "Timer." Set your desired countdown time, pause it if needed, or cancel and reset. Customize the alert tone when the timer reaches zero.

Tip: Utilize Siri for quick timer setup. Just say "Hey Siri, start the timer" or press the side button and say "Start timer" to initiate it effortlessly.

COMPASS

The Compass app  is a handy tool that provides you with directions, coordinates, and elevation data for your current location. To access it, simply tap on the Compass app icon , and your iPhone will display all the relevant information about your location on your screen.

Additionally, the Compass app can assist you in maintaining a particular direction. By tapping the dial, you can set it to a specific direction, and whenever you deviate from that course, it will display a red band to indicate how far off you are from your intended heading.

Furthermore, you can easily view the location corresponding to your current coordinates on Maps by tapping the coordinates displayed beneath the compass. This feature allows for seamless navigation and exploration.

CONTACT

The Contact app ⊙ on your iPhone is designed to keep your contact information private, secure, and backed up. It provides a centralized location to store and access the numbers, emails, and addresses of your contacts.

ADDING OR UPDATING CONTACTS IS STRAIGHTFORWARD:

1. Open the Contact app ⊙ and tap the ✛ button.
2. Enter the contact's information, including their name, number, email, and more. You can also add photos to contacts by tapping the photo icon.
3. To include multiple numbers, emails, or addresses, tap the ✛ symbol and choose labels or create custom ones.
4. Tap "Done" at the top-right corner to save the contact.

TO ACCESS AND UPDATE CONTACT DETAILS:

1. Navigate to the Contact app ⊙ and tap on a contact to view their information.
2. Use the quick task buttons below the contact photo for actions like Message, Call, FaceTime, Mail, and Pay (via Apple Pay).

TO EDIT CONTACT INFORMATION:

1. Tap "Edit" at the top-right corner.
2. Modify or delete information by tapping ⊕ or ⊖ .
3. Tap "Done" to save the changes.

Your iPhone also creates a contact card called "My Card" for you, which can be used for Autofill on websites and forms. To set up "My Card":
1. Tap "My Card" at the top of your contact list.
2. Enter your contact information and tap "Done" to save it.

If you don't see "My Card" at the top of your contact app, you can manually create it in Settings:
1. Tap the ✛ button and enter your information.
2. To make it "My Card," go to Settings > Contacts > My Info, and select the contact you

just saved.

For secure, backed-up, and synchronized contacts, you can use iCloud:

1. Go to Settings 🌐 > Your Name.
2. Tap "iCloud" and enable the contact toggle to sync your contacts across all your devices.

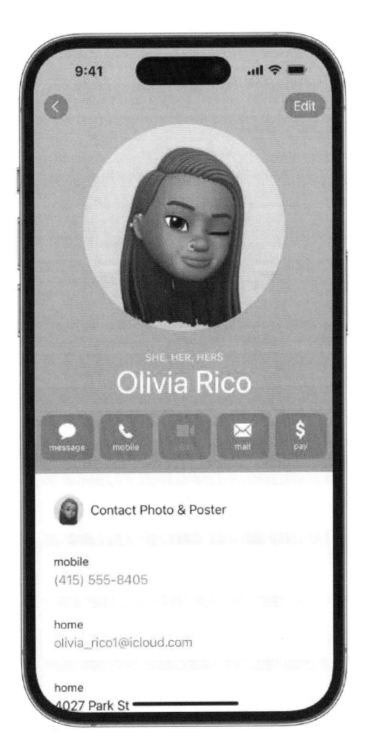

FACETIME

FaceTime is a versatile feature on your iPhone that allows for both audio and video calls with your contacts. It goes beyond simple communication by enabling you to share your screen and various types of content with friends and family during a call. Whether you want to watch movies, share music, show photos, or explore web pages, FaceTime provides real-time interactions and reactions to your shared content.

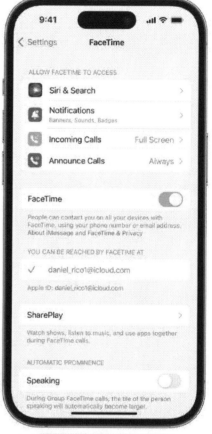

TO SET UP FACETIME

1. 1. Go to Settings and tap "FaceTime."
2. 2. Turn on the FaceTime button. Within settings, you can customize notification settings, choose your Caller ID, and specify how people can contact you on FaceTime, whether through your Apple ID or phone number.

Making or receiving FaceTime calls is as straightforward as regular calls. You can engage in individual or group video and audio calls using your phone number or Apple ID, requiring only your iPhone and an active internet connection.

TO MAKE A FACETIME CALL

1. Open FaceTime and tap "New FaceTime" on your screen.
2. If you're new to FaceTime, select a contact from suggestions or tap the button to add a contact for a FaceTime call.
3. After making the call, it will appear in your list of recent calls within the FaceTime app. For subsequent calls to the same contact, tap their name or use the button from your recent FaceTime call log.

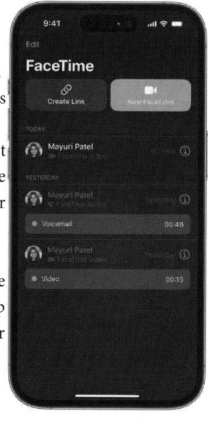

Additionally, you can initiate a FaceTime call directly from the Messages app. Within a message thread with your contact, tap the camera or phone con to choose between an audio or video call.

During a FaceTime call, you'll find various controls on your screen to enhance your call experience. Here's a breakdown of these controls:

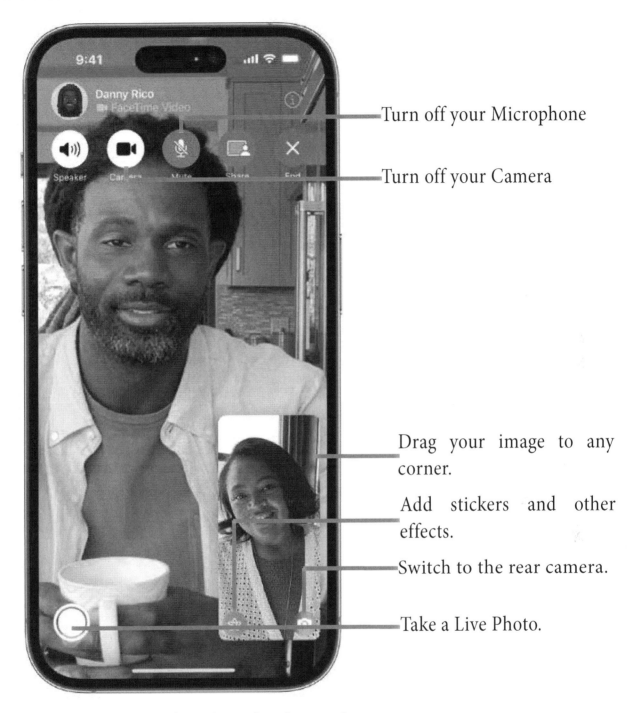

Turn off your Microphone

Turn off your Camera

Drag your image to any corner.

Add stickers and other effects.

Switch to the rear camera.

Take a Live Photo.

To make a group call with your friends or family members:

1. Open FaceTime ▢ and tap "New FaceTime" on your screen.
2. Tap the ⊕ button to add contacts. You can include up to 32 participants in a single group call.
3. Choose between an audio or video group call by tapping the microphone 📞 or camera ▢ icon.

In a group call, all participants will be displayed as tiles on your screen. The tile of the active speaker becomes more prominent when they are speaking, helping you identify the current speaker. If you have too many participants to fit on the screen, some will appear on the screen while the rest are displayed in a row at the bottom of your call screen. You can swipe through the row to see all participants.

Receiving a FaceTime call is similar to receiving a regular call on your iPhone. You can tap "Answer" to accept the call or "Decline" by tapping the red button to decline it. There are also options to decline the call and set a reminder for a callback or send a quick message using available message templates.

ENHANCE VIDEO CALLS WITH MEMOJI, FILTERS, TEXT, STICKERS, AND MORE

To make your video calls more fun and engaging, FaceTime offers various effects. You can add text, stickers, memojis, and other fun effects to your video call. These effects are visible to all participants, and they can also apply effects of their own, creating an interactive and enjoyable call experience.

PORTRAIT MODE

FaceTime offers portrait modes to enhance your video calls. You can blur your call background, creating a photographic or cinematic effect with the focus solely on you.

To apply the portrait mode effect during a call, simply tap your tile on the screen, then tap to toggle portrait mode on and off during the call.

Turn Portrait mode off or on.

Tap 🔄 to switch to the rear camera and show your surroundings to the caller. Tap it again to switch back to the front camera. For added fun, you can apply exciting filters to your call by tapping ✴ on your tile and selecting from the following options:

MEMOJI

Utilizing the Face ID camera, your emojis can now mirror your facial expressions and movements in real-time. These animated emojis, known as Memoji, can be used in both the Message app and FaceTime.

To add Memoji to your FaceTime call:
1. Tap your tile and then select for more options.
2. Tap to see the available characters you can use as your Memoji. Select your preferred character, and it will appear as your face in the FaceTime video call.

FILTERS

Filters alter your appearance on camera by adding various colors and effects to your video during a FaceTime call.

To apply and change filters during your call:
1. Tap your tile and then select for more options.
2. Tap and then simply choose the filter you'd like to apply to your video call.

TEXT LABELS

Text labels are essentially the text you type that appears on the call screen. After entering the desired text in the provided space, you can place it anywhere on your screen. The same can be done by your participant, and the text will appear on both screens.

To add text labels to your calls:
1. Tap your tile and then select for more options.
2. Tap to view and select the text label option displayed on your screen.
3. Type the text in your chosen label. To reposition it on the screen, tap outside the text box or placeholder, then move the text with your fingers.
4. If you want to remove your text, tap your text label and then select to remove it from the screen.

SHAPES

FaceTime offers various shapes that you can use in your video for different purposes.

To add shapes:

1. Tap your tile and then select ⊛ for more options.
2. Tap ⬢ to view and choose any shape you'd like to add to your video.
3. To remove the shape, first, tap the shape and then select.

STICKERS

Similar to text labels or shapes, you can add Memoji stickers or Emoji stickers. These can be placed anywhere on your screen.

To add a Memoji or Emoji sticker:
1. Tap your tile and then select ⊛ for more options.
2. Tap ▣ to add an emoji sticker on the screen or tap ⬢ to add a Memoji sticker.
3. Tap and drag the sticker on the screen to place it wherever you'd like.
4. Tap the sticker and then select ⊗ to remove it from your screen.

SHARE SCREEN OR VIDEOS & MUSIC USING SHAREPLAY

With screen sharing, you can now show your friends content in real-time during a video call. This feature makes your calls more interactive and enjoyable. To share your screen during a call, tap the screen to reveal all video call controls. Then, select ▣ and choose "Share My Screen." Your screen will be shared with everyone on the call after a three-second countdown. You can open your gallery to display photos and albums, open Safari to share web pages, or use other apps from your home screen to engage with your participants.

SHAREPLAY

While screen sharing allows you to share photos, albums, and webpages, SharePlay takes it a step further by enabling you to watch movies and listen to music together. When using SharePlay, the video and audio will be synchronized across all participants' screens. To utilize SharePlay during your call, open a streaming app that supports this feature, such as Apple TV 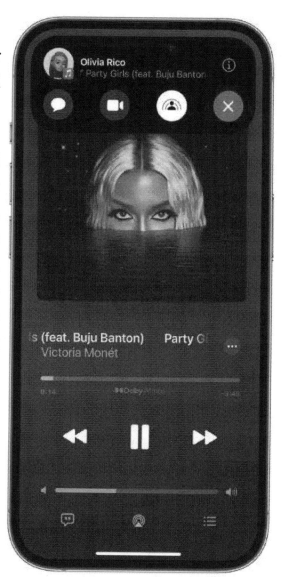, the Music app 🎵, or the App Store. Start playing the content on your screen and tap "Play for Everyone." This option will only appear when the app supports SharePlay.

Once the screen is shared, every participant will have access to music and video controls on their screen. This allows them to pause, play, fast forward, or rewind the content being displayed. If a single participant uses any control on their screen, it will also affect the other screens. For instance, if one participant pauses the movie or music, it will pause on all participants' devices simultaneously, ensuring that the content remains synchronized.

It's worth noting that in some apps, both you and the other participant may need to have a subscription. Additionally, SharePlay availability may vary by region. If you're unable to access the SharePlay feature, please check the availability in your country by visiting the Apple website, as the feature may not be available in all countries.

FILES

The Files app is a versatile tool that creates folders and provides cloud storage for your documents and data on iCloud, ensuring seamless updates across all your iOS devices linked to your Apple ID. With the Files app, you can conveniently access and share all your files from a single location.

Furthermore, the Files app offers the flexibility to connect external drives, including USB devices, SD cards, and other storage devices, directly to your iOS device.

ICLOUD DRIVE

To make the most of iCloud Drive and enable your phone to access and synchronize data via iCloud across all devices, follow these steps to set up iCloud Drive:

1. Navigate to Settings > Tap on your Name > Tap on "iCloud."
2. Toggle on the "iCloud Drive" option to enable cloud storage for storing and sharing files.

iCloud Drive provides a platform to organize, modify, and share your documents and data. Within the Files app, you'll find various options to access and share your data effectively.

1. Open the Files app and tap "Browse" at the top-left corner of your screen. Here, you'll encounter the following available options:

- On My iPhone: This section displays all the data stored in various apps on your iPhone. To grant iCloud permission to access this data, go to Settings > Tap on your Name > Tap "iCloud" and enable the apps you wish to access via iCloud in the Files app.
- iCloud Drive: This drive acts as a central hub for storing and syncing your files across all your devices using your Apple ID. You can manage, edit, and share files and folders directly from the app. Within iCloud Drive, when you tap you can:
  - Organize: Sort your files and folders by name, size, date, type, or change the view between grid and list forms.

- Add Folders: Create new folders to store and categorize files as needed.

- Scanning Documents: If you have a document that needs scanning and subsequent uploading, editing, or sharing, utilize the "Scan Document" feature. To work with scanned documents or those already in your drive:

    - Tap to access the scanned document or any document that's already part of your drive.

    - Tap the ⚫⚫⚫ icon to initiate editing and sharing options.

    - Alternatively, select the signature icon Ⓐ or markup tool to add your signature or annotations.

    - To share the document, tap the share icon ⬆ and choose to send it via messages or other compatible apps.

ACCESS EXTERNAL STORAGE AND SERVERS IN FILES

The Files app supports connecting external storage devices like SD cards, USB drives, and various cloud storage services, such as Google Drive or Dropbox. Additionally, you can establish connections with online servers directly from your iPhone.

To access external storage or servers in Files:
1. Open the Files app 📁 and tap "Browse."
2. Tap ⚫⚫⚫ to reveal more options, then select "Connect to Server."
3. On the following screen, choose whether you're joining as a "Guest" or "Registered User." Provide your username and password if connecting as a "Registered User." To disconnect your iPhone from the server, go to the "Browse" screen in the Files app and tap ⏏ the "Disconnect" option displayed next to the server name.

For cloud storage services other than iCloud, like Google Drive, download the respective app from the App Store and set it up by signing in. Go to the Files app, tap "Browse," select "More Locations" from the list, and enable your external cloud storage services to make them accessible within the Files app.

For external storage devices such as SD cards, USB drives, or external hard drives, you'll need USB type C cable, which can be obtained from an Apple Store. Plug your external storage into the USB side to your iPhone's port. Open the Files app and go to "Browse" to access and manage your external drive.

FIND MY APP

The Find My app 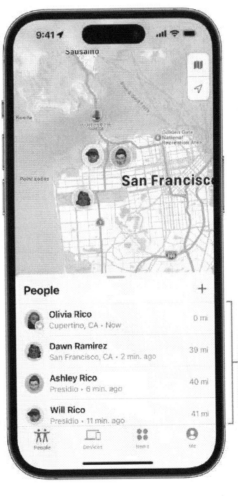 is a powerful tool that allows you to track the locations of devices associated with your Apple ID, as well as the locations of friends and family members who have been added using their Apple IDs or phone numbers. This app helps you locate lost devices, enable security measures such as device locking, and even play sounds to help you find your devices.

Setting up Find My: To configure Find My, navigate to Settings > Your Name > Find My , and toggle the feature on.

FRIENDS AND FAMILY LOCATION SHARING:

To add friends and family members to your Find My list, ensure that your location services are active, and your phone has permission to share your location with them. To share your location and add others:

1. Go to Find My > Tap "Me" at the bottom of your screen.
2. Activate "Share My Location."
3. To add people, go to Find My > Tap "People" > Tap "Share My Location" to send them a location-sharing request.
4. Once they accept your request, both parties can view each other's locations.
5. To stop sharing with someone, tap their name and select "Stop Sharing Location," confirming the action.
6. To remove someone from your list, tap their name and choose "Remove," confirming the removal.

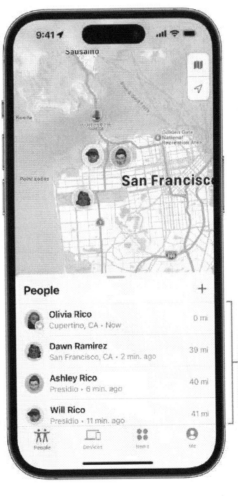

Tap a person to see contact information, get directions, and more.

TRACKING DEVICES AND ITEMS

Find My keeps tabs on all your devices signed in with your Apple ID, as well as accessories connected to these devices (such as AirPods and third-party items). Access your devices and accessories by going to Find My and tapping "Devices." To add devices, tap ➕ then:

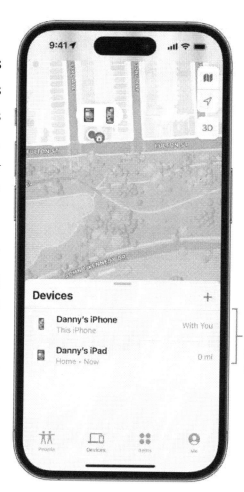

Tap a device to play a sound, get directions, and more.

- Tap any device to access Find My options, including directions, playing a sound, or marking the device as lost.

- "Play Sound" helps you locate a nearby device by playing a sound.

- Enable "Notifications" to receive alerts when your devices are separated from you.

LOST DEVICE

If a device is lost, use "Mark As Lost" to secure it with a message displaying your contact information or lock it for added security.

The "Items" category includes other belongings like keys, wallets, and purses, which can be tracked using AirTags connected to your iPhone. You can access precise locations and additional options to secure your items.

HEALTH APP

Your iPhone's Health app is a powerful tool for tracking your daily activities and improving your overall health. It records your activity data and stores it securely on your iCloud. This includes tracking steps taken, floors climbed, and various exercises you've completed, which can be recorded automatically, manually, or imported from your Apple Watch.

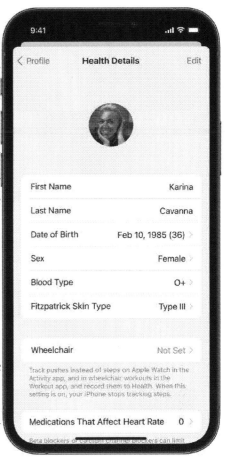

CREATING YOUR PROFILE & MEDICAL ID

To set up your profile and Medical ID in the Health app:

1. Open the Health app 🤍 and tap your profile icon in the top-right corner.
2. Tap "Health Details" and input relevant information about your general health.

Your Medical ID serves as a vital resource in emergencies, as it contains information about your body measurements and any existing health conditions. Medical ID can be accessed from the lock screen, providing first responders with essential details such as allergies, medical conditions, and contact information.

To access or update your Medical ID, go to the Health app 🤍, tap your profile, and then select "Medical ID."

Note: First responders can access your Medical ID by swiping from the bottom to the top on the passcode screen, tapping "Emergency" in the bottom-left corner, and then selecting "Medical ID" on the dialer screen.

MONITORING YOUR ACTIVITY

The Health app offers an easy-to-read activity summary that highlights various categories, including walking, workouts, and energy burned. Each category provides a quick overview of your daily activities.

- To view this summary, open the Health app and tap "Summary" at the bottom of your screen.

- You can customize the activity highlights by tapping "Edit" on the next screen to add or remove categories.

If your phone misses any important activity data, you can manually add it by selecting the relevant activity category and tapping "Add Data" in the top right corner.

The Health app 💚 helps you stay active and healthy by displaying your health trends and suggesting additional activities. To explore health trends and detailed information for specific categories:

- Tap "Browse" at the bottom of your screen.
- Select an activity to view its details. For instance, you can track your cardio activity over various timeframes, such as a day, week, month, or year, by tapping "Mobility" to access the data.

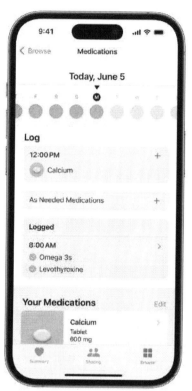

MANAGE YOUR MEDICATIONS

Keep track of the drugs you're prescribed and schedule when to take them with ease. You can even log when you've taken them. Adding a new medication is simple. Just follow these steps:

1. Tap "Browse."
2. Select "Medications."
3. Tap "Add a Medication."

MONITOR YOUR MENSTRUAL CYCLE

Cycle Tracking is a great feature for monitoring your menstrual cycle. Record symptoms like cramps and track cycle-related factors such as lactation. This feature can even help predict the onset of your next period or fertile window. To set up Cycle Tracking, follow these steps:

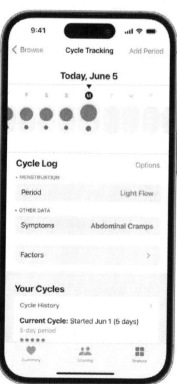

1. Tap "Browse."
2. Choose "Cycle Tracking."
3. Select "Set Up Cycle Tracking."

ITUNES STORE

The iTunes Store 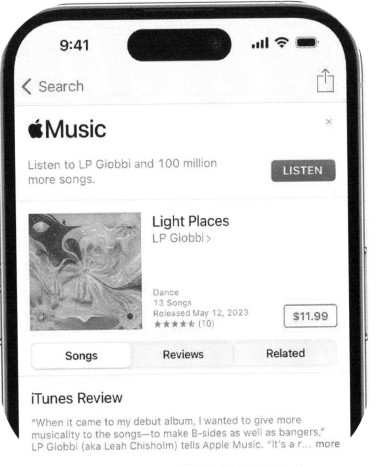 is your one-stop shop for all your favorite music, movies, and TV shows. You can buy and download your preferred content directly from the app. Once purchased and downloaded, you can access it anytime on your iPhone.

To navigate the iTunes Store app, follow these steps:

1. Open the iTunes Store app on your device.
2. Explore the various categories available on your screen. You can tap on the following options:

   - Music: This category is where you can find your favorite songs and albums.

   - Movies: Here, you can discover and purchase movies to watch on your device.

   - TV Shows: Access a wide range of TV shows available for purchase.

   - Charts: Discover trending and popular content in the charts section.

   - Search: Use the search function to find specific content of your choice.

   - More: Tap on "More" to access personalized recommendations based on your previous purchases.

3. To make a purchase, simply tap on the price of any music track, movie, or TV show that you want to buy. Follow the on-screen instructions to complete the payment process. If you see a cloud icon instead of a price, it means you've already purchased it, and you can download it again at no additional cost.

4. In addition to music, movies, and TV shows, you can also download and purchase new notification tones, including incoming call ringtones, text tones, and other alert tones. To buy new notification tones:

- Tap "More" within the iTunes Store app.

- Select "Tones" to explore the available notification tones.

- Use the "Search" function to quickly locate the specific tone you're looking for.

- If it's a paid tone, tap the price to initiate the purchase.

MANAGING AND VIEWING YOUR PURCHASES ON THE ITUNES STORE

In the iTunes Store, tap "More" and go to "Purchase." Here, you'll find a record of all your purchases made on the iTunes Store on your device. You can also review billing information, receive email receipts for your purchases, and report any issues with previous transactions.

In the "Purchase" section, you'll see all the content you've bought with your Apple ID in the iTunes store. If you want to re-download any previous purchase, simply tap the cloud icon to retrieve the content back to your phone.

MAIL

You can conveniently send and receive emails directly from your iPhone using the Mail app. The Mail app offers a variety of tools to compose and send professional and personal emails, allowing you to attach photos and videos, use different text formatting options, styles, bullet points, and more to create engaging emails.

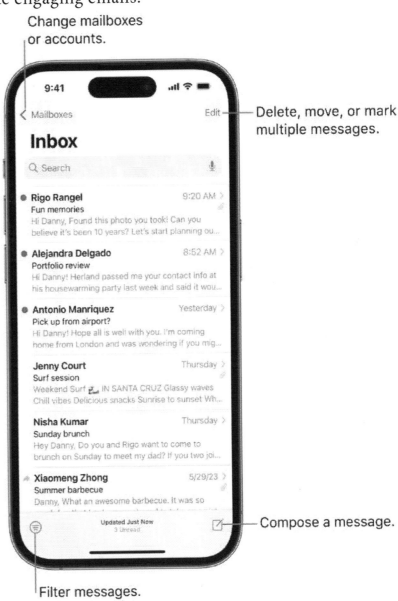

Change mailboxes or accounts.

Delete, move, or mark multiple messages.

Compose a message.

Filter messages.

SET UP YOUR MAIL APP

- Open the Mail app 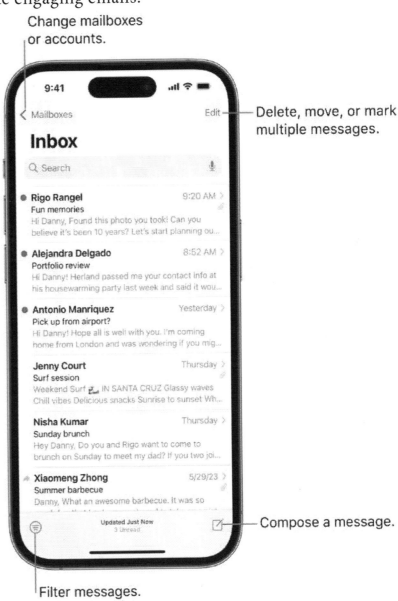 on your iPhone.

- Choose which email account you want to set up from the provided list. For example, if you have a Gmail account, select "Google" and enter your login information to set up the Mail app.

- If you want to add multiple accounts, go to "Settings" > tap "Mail" > tap "Accounts" > then choose "Add Account" and provide the login information for each account.

COMPOSE OR REPLY TO EMAILS

- To compose a new email, tap the pen icon ☑ to start a new email.

- If you want to reply to an email you've received, tap the email in your inbox, then tap the arrow icon ↩ to write a reply.

- Enter the recipient's email address at the top, or tap the "Add" button ⊕ to add an email address from your contacts.

- In the "Cc" field, you can send copies to additional recipients. In "Bcc," you can send copies to multiple recipients without revealing their addresses to others.

- Enter your subject and compose your email. Once you're finished, tap the send icon ⬆ to send your email.

TEXT FORMATTING AND ATTACHMENTS

- While composing an email, you can change the formatting of text, add bullet points, and more by tapping ‹ the format bar located above your keyboard.

- Use the icons to add photos 🖼 or videos ◙ from your gallery, take new pictures and videos, format text Aa, and add attachments or documents to your email.

- For PDFs and other files, tap the paperclip icon ▱ and choose a document from your location. You can also scan a new document ▣, crop it, add filters, and then attach it to your email.

- Additionally, you can add drawings to your email by tapping the pencil icon Ⓐ, drawing, and then inserting the drawing into the email.

MANAGE YOUR MAILBOXES

To manage your mailboxes, tap ‹ on the top-left corner of your screen in the mail app. Once you are on the mailboxes screen, tap "Edit" at the top-right corner of your screen. Tap any of the Inboxes to add it your mailboxes or tap and hold the ☰ to move the mailbox up or below its position in the list. Tap "Done" to finish organizing your mailboxes.

MAPS

Utilize the Maps app 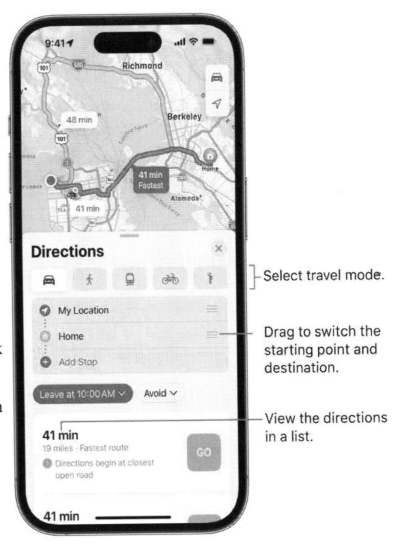 to discover nearby locations. Maps can assist you in obtaining directions to your favourite restaurants, shopping centers, and various other establishments in your vicinity. You can also gather information about new destinations you intend to visit by perusing reviews from individuals who have previously explored and shared their insights.

ENABLE LOCATION SERVICES

- To allow Maps to use your location for navigation, ensure that Location Services are enabled on your iPhone. Go to "Settings" > "Privacy" > "Location Services," and then toggle them on. Scroll down and find "Maps" in the list of apps; make sure it's set to "While Using the App" for optimal functionality.

EXPLORE MAPS CONTROLS

- When you open the Maps app, you will see various controls on your screen:

- Tap the location icon to center the map on your current location with north at the top of your screen.

- Tap the location icon with a directional arrow to show your current location without locking north at the top.

- Tap the directional arrow to lock north at the top.

- Below the location controls, you can choose different types of maps:

- Exploring, Driving, Public Transport, and Satellite.

- You can switch between 2D and 3D views for different map perspectives.

Select travel mode.

Drag to switch the starting point and destination.

View the directions in a list.

FIND DIRECTIONS

- To get directions to a specific place, tap the search bar at the top and enter the name of the destination (e.g., a restaurant or gym).
- Maps can also show nearby places. To explore your surroundings, tap the search bar and browse categories under the "Nearby" section. Select the category or type the name of the place you want directions to.
- After selecting a place, you'll see information about it, including a description, address, contact details, and reviews.
- Tap the "Direction Button" to set a route to your destination. Maps may provide multiple route options; tap an alternative route to switch between them.

PIN A PLACE

You can drop a pin on the map to mark a location you want to follow directions to or share with others. To pin a location:

- Find the destination or place by searching or exploring the map.
- Tap and hold the location on your screen to drop a pin.
- After dropping the pin, you can adjust its location by moving it or zooming in for precision.
- Tap ••• for more options, including adding it to your favorites or sharing it.

BOOK A RIDE

Maps can integrate with ride-booking apps like Uber or Didi, allowing you to book rides directly from the app. To book a ride in Maps:

- Download the compatible ride-booking apps from the App Store if you haven't already.
- In Maps, search for your destination and tap "Direction."
- Tap the ride-sharing icon 🕴 to book a ride, and the app will suggest the best options for you based on availability and pricing.

MESSAGES

The Messages app ⬜ brings an element of enjoyment and productivity to your regular texting routine with its entertaining effects, photo and video sharing capabilities. Additionally, it supports Apple Pay for quick money transfers with your contacts and integrates seamlessly with apps like Maps and other third-party location services, allowing you to instantly share your whereabouts with friends and family.

IMESSAGES

iMessages, specifically designed for iPhone users, distinguish themselves with blue message bubbles when exchanged between iPhones and green when communicating with non-iPhone users. These messages can be sent and received via Wi-Fi or cellular connections. If you attempt to send an iMessage without an internet connection, your iPhone will automatically convert it into a regular text message.

To set up iMessages, navigate to Settings ⚙ > Messages and activate the "iMessages" option. Just below iMessage settings, access "Send & Receive" to determine whether you want to utilize your email address or phone number for sending and receiving messages.

You can opt to store your text messages and iMessages on iCloud, ensuring that your message history remains accessible across multiple devices. To enable this feature, visit Settings ⚙ > Your Name > iCloud, and toggle on the "Messages" option.

STARTING A CONVERSATION

Initiating a conversation in the Messages app is a breeze. Here's how to get started:

1. Open the Messages app ⬜ and tap the ✏ icon at the top-right of your screen.
2. To perform additional actions such as deleting multiple conversations or pinning a conversation to the top of your list, tap "Edit."
3. Type the contact's name you want to message or tap the icon to select from your contact list.
4. Enter your message in the message bar and then tap the send icon. If the message bubble appears blue, it means you are sending an iMessage. If it's green, you're sending a regular text message.

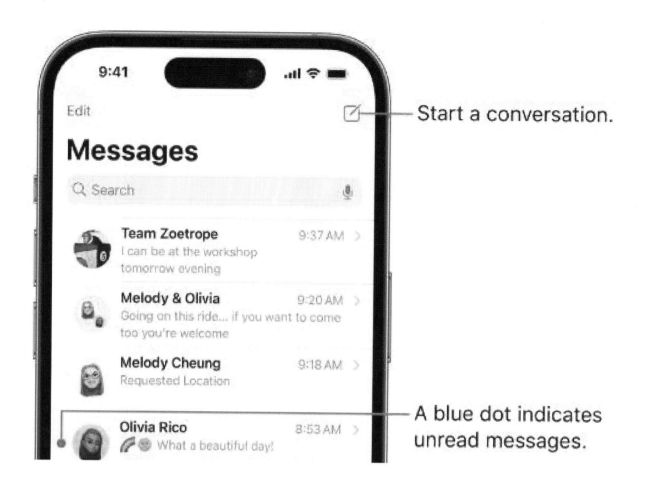

Start a conversation.

A blue dot indicates unread messages.

You can also initiate a FaceTime call directly from your conversation in the Messages app. While in a conversation, tap the icon at the top-right of your conversation and choose whether you want to make an audio or video call.

ENHANCE YOUR MESSAGES WITH BUBBLE & SCREEN EFFECTS

You can add effects to your message bubble or message screen, which is especially fun when sending iMessages from one iPhone to another. Both you and your recipient can send and receive these effects. When you receive a message with effects, it will automatically play the applied effect.

TO APPLY BUBBLE OR SCREEN EFFECTS

1. Type your message.
2. Tap and hold the ⬆ button.
3. Choose from various effects. Tap "Bubble" to apply effects to your message bubble or "Screen" for effects on your message screen.

TO SEND PHOTOS, VIDEOS, OR AUDIO MESSAGES

1. Tap the bar just above your keyboard.

2. Tap 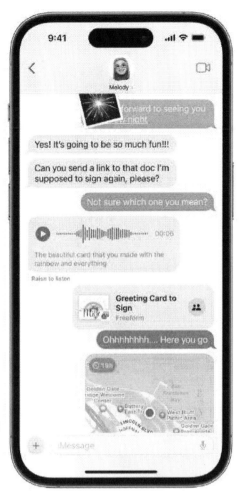 to capture a new photo or video to add to your conversation. Choose the photo or video mode and then tap the capture button. Send it by tapping the send button at the lower-left corner. You can also edit, add effects, or markups before sending.

3. To add photos or videos from your iPhone gallery, tap . Choose a photo or video, and then tap to send it. You can edit, add markups, or apply effects before sending.

4. For audio messages, tap to record your message. You can listen to it before sending by tapping . If it's ready to send, tap . If you want to re-record, tap .

To listen to an audio message received, tap the message you want to hear and then tap play or raise your phone to your ear for automatic playback.

You can save photos and videos received in iMessage to your gallery. In iMessage, tap the save button next to the photos or videos sent or received.

CREATE AND SEND MEMOJI STICKERS, VIDEOS, AND DIGITAL EFFECTS

1. Memoji: These are animated emoji faces with expressions from your own face.

   • While in a conversation, tap and then tap + button to create a Memoji.

   • Customize your Memoji by choosing skin tone, hairstyle, facial hair, and more to match your looks.

   • Tap "Done" to add your Memoji to your collection. You can use it in other conversations too.

   • To send Memoji stickers, tap and then select the Memoji you want to send.

2. Memoji Videos: Record live videos with your Memoji expressions.

- Tap  just above your keyboard.

- Choose the character for your face in the video and tap ⬤ to start recording with your facial expressions.

- Tap ⓞ to send the recorded Memoji video or 🗑 to cancel and re-record.

3. Digital Stickers:

- Open the Messages app ⬜ on your iPhone and either start a new message or open a conversation.

- Tap the ◐ icon then tap ╋.

- Choose a photo from your camera roll that you'd like to turn into a sticker.

- If you want a still image sticker, tap "Add Sticker." If you want a moving Live Sticker, use a Live Photo instead.

- To add an effect, hold down on the sticker and tap "Add Effect," then select an option.

- Once you're happy with your sticker, you can save it to your favorites or share it with friends and family stickers.

MUSIC

Apple Music 🎵 is your gateway to the latest global music offerings. With millions of ad-free songs, you can stream, download, or enjoy various radio stations right from your Music app.

APPLE MUSIC SUBSCRIPTION

To indulge in your favorite music on your iPhone, an active subscription to Apple Music is necessary. Open your Music app to subscribe. The available plans and instructions will be shown when you open the Music app for the first time. Alternatively, you can go to Settings ⚙ > tap "Music" > tap "Subscriptions" to view and select a plan.

Additionally, you can directly download music from the iTunes Store and enjoy it in the Music app. Search for your preferred music, purchase, and then either stream or download for offline listening.

For subscription management, go to the Music app 🎵 > tap "Your Profile" (top-right) > tap "Manage Subscriptions" to modify or cancel your Apple Music plan.

After subscribing, you're all set to explore your preferred music. Tap "Browse" at the bottom of your screen in the Music app to discover and download new music across various genres.

CONTROLS ON YOUR MUSIC APP

To enjoy your purchased and downloaded music on your iPhone, follow these steps:

1. Tap "Library" located at the bottom of your screen within the Music app.

2. Within your library, you can explore various categories to find a specific song or artist from your collection of stored music.

3. Additionally, you have the option to create personalized playlists and queues to match your music with your mood and preferences.

Once you've selected a song from your music library, you can utilize the following controls within the Music app:

- Tap the play button to start playing the most recent song in your music collection.

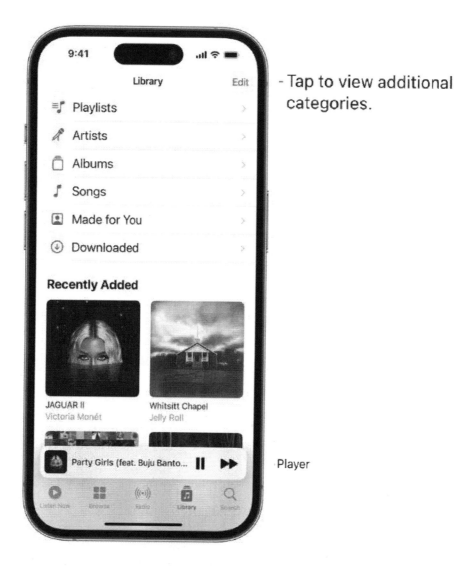

- Tap to view additional categories.

Player

Tap any of the songs in your music library and then use the following controls in your Music app:

 Tap it to play the recent song on your player.

 Pause the music that you are listening to.

 Tap once to play the next song on the playlist or queue. Tap and hold to fast-forward your current song.

Tap once to return to the current song's beginning then tap again to play previous song. Tap and hold to rewind a song.

 While in a queue, tap it once to repeat the song at the end of the queue and tap it again to repeat a single track.

 Open queue and then tap the shuffle button to let the song play in a random order in your player.

 Tap for more options.

 Tap it to minimize your player in the Music app.

 It shows time-synced lyrics on your Music app screen as the song plays.

 Listen and stream music on Bluetooth & AirPlay devices connected to your phone.

 Tap the button to see and organize songs in the queue

To control volume and duration for your music manually, you can use the sliders on the screen. You can also choose how your music sound on your iPhone's speakers. iPhone gives you a different option to make your music sound the best. Go to Settings ⚙ > tap "Music" and then choose "EQ." Change it to your what best suits your preferred music.

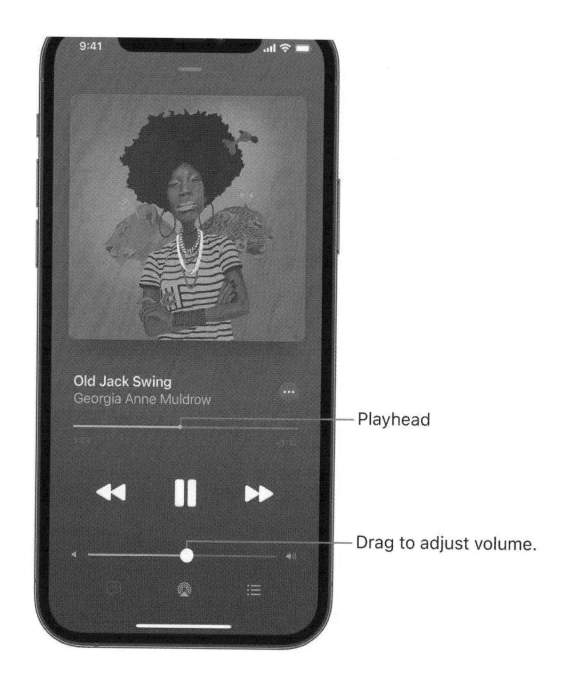

Playhead

Drag to adjust volume.

To listen to your purchased and downloaded music on your iPhone, tap "Library" from the bar at bottom of your screen.

In the library, tap any category to find a song or artist from music stored on your iPhone.

You can also create your own personalized playlists and queues to play music to your moods.

NEWS

The News app ▨ is your gateway to the latest updates and stories on topics you care about, sourced from some of the world's most reputable and popular outlets. It gathers and organizes these stories in your app and even on your home screen through a convenient widget, ensuring you stay informed about the events and subjects that pique your interest. The app's algorithms also make tailored content recommendations based on your reading habits, improving its suggestions the more you read.

If you're eager to delve into even more premium content, you can subscribe to Apple News+ within the News app. This subscription grants you access to a wealth of premium magazines, newspapers, and top publishers from around the globe.

GET STARTED & PERSONALIZE YOUR NEWSFEED

1. Open the News app ▨ to kick off your news-reading journey. You'll see news stories from various topics and sources displayed on your app's screen.

2. To start following your favorite sources and channels, tap "Following" located at the bottom of the screen. Then, simply tap the ⊕ icon next to the channel you want to follow.

3. If you're interested in discovering new channels or searching for specific ones, head to the "Discover" section. Here, you can browse for channels that catch your eye and tap the ⊕ icon to follow them. Alternatively, use the "Search" function to find and follow specific channels.

4. If you ever wish to unfollow a topic, channel, or publication, go to the "Following" section. Swipe left on the name of the topic, channel, or publication you want to unfollow, and then tap "Unfollow."

5. To manage notifications for the topics and channels you follow, navigate to your iPhone's Settings ⚙, tap "News," then select "Restrict Stories in Today." Confirm your choices to tailor your notification preferences for news stories.

For Apple News+ subscribers, you can enjoy premium stories and content right within the News app. Access top-tier publishers, magazines, and news stories across various topics.

APPLE NEWS+

1. Here's how to subscribe to Apple News+:

2. Open the News app ⬛ .

3. Tap on any magazine or paid channel you'd like to subscribe to.

4. Look for the "Subscription" button within that magazine, channel, or publication, and tap it.

5. Follow the on-screen instructions to complete your subscription for the selected publisher or magazine. With Apple News+, you have the option to download stories to your iPhone for later reading.

1. Should you ever wish to cancel your subscription:

2. Navigate to the "Following" section within the News app.

3. Scroll to the bottom and tap "Subscription."

4. Follow the on-screen instructions to cancel any subscription associated with your Apple News+.

Additionally, the News app offers audio news, perfect for staying updated on the go when you're short on time for reading. Simply tap the audio icon 🎧 and explore the stories available for listening. Tap on the story you want to hear, and the app will begin playing it. Use the audio controls to adjust the volume, speed, and other audio-related features to enhance your listening experience.

NOTES

The Notes app ⬚ is your versatile tool for jotting down everything from grocery lists to safeguarding your private information. It provides multiple ways to record and secure your data, with the added benefit of seamless synchronization through iCloud to ensure your notes are safe and up-to-date.

CREATE NEW NOTES

To create a new note in the app, open Notes ⬚, tap the ✏️ symbol at the bottom of your screen, and begin typing your new note. If you want to format, style, or add attachments, follow these steps:

TABLES

Tap the table icon ⊞ to insert tables into your notes. Touch any cell to start typing content. To add or delete columns and rows, tap the selection handle. To delete the entire table, tap any cell and then tap ⊞ to access more options, including copy, delete, share, or convert the table into simple text.

CHECKLISTS

Tap the checklist icon ☑ to create a checklist for recording and organizing items in your notes. You can add or remove items, mark them as checked, and manually or automatically sort them. To automatically sort checked items, go to Settings ⚙ > Notes > Sort Checked Items and turn on "Automatically."

FORMATTING

Tap the formatting icon Aa to add titles, headings, subheadings, bullet points, and styling features to your notes. To format existing text, select the text and then tap Aa to apply the desired formatting.

ATTACHMENTS

Tap the attachment icon 📷 and choose to take a new photo, select one from your gallery, or scan a document ⬚ to add to your note. You can scan and add text directly from a document within the Notes app.

DRAWING

Tap the drawing icon ⒶⒶ to create sketches, shapes, or other drawings within your notes. You can use various tools like colors, markers, pencils, and rulers to enhance your drawings.

Once you're done, tap "Done" at the top-right corner to save your notes. You can also enhance the security of your private notes by locking them. While editing the note, tap ⋯ and then tap lock. The iPhone may ask you to set the password for notes. Go to Settings ⚙ > Tap "Notes" and then tap "Password" to set a new password for your private notes.

ORGANIZE YOUR NOTES USING TAGS & SMART FOLDERS

FOLDERS

1. Open the Notes app and locate the folder icon 🗁 positioned at the bottom-left corner, just beneath the folder list.
2. You'll be presented with two options: "New Folder" and "New Smart Folder."
3. A smart folder is designed to automatically categorize notes based on tags you assign to them. When you add a tag to a note, it will be included in the corresponding smart folder.

TAGS

1. To attach a tag to your notes, simply input "#" followed by the tag name (e.g., #work, #personal) without any spaces.
2. Notes will recognize the tag and highlight it, placing it within the Tags section under the folder list.
3. If you wish to delete or alter a tag, tap on the tag itself, allowing you to remove or modify it as needed.

SORTING

1. For customizing the order of your folders, tap "Edit" found at the top-right corner.
2. This will enable you to arrange your folders in a sequence that suits your preferences.

To ensure your notes are securely backed up and synchronized across multiple iOS devices, follow these steps:

1. Access your device's Settings .
2. Scroll down and tap on your personal profile, usually indicated by your name.
3. In the following menu, select "iCloud."
4. Switch on the "Notes" option.

If you prefer to use alternate accounts, such as your Google account, for backing up your notes, these steps will guide you:

1. Open the Settings  on your device.

2. Locate the "Notes" section.

3. Choose "Accounts."

4. Opt for your desired account to serve as the default option for storing your notes.

5. Should you want to retain your notes exclusively on your iPhone them to iCloud, activate the "On My iPhone" account option.

SCAN TEXT

If you want to add a piece of paper to your note, you can use your phone's camera. First, click on "Scan Text" in the note and make sure your phone is pointing at the paper. Then, select the text you want and tap "Insert".

SCAN A DOCUMENT

If you need to scan a whole document, click on "Scan Documents" an at the page. Your phone will take a picture automatically, but you can if you need to. If there are more pages, scan them too and click "Save" The document will be saved in your note as a PDF.

PHONE

The Phone app on your iPhone is your hub for managing call logs, voicemails, contacts, and, of course, making calls. Here's a step-by-step guide on how to use the Phone app efficiently:

MAKING A CALL OR SAVING A CONTACT

1. Open the Phone app .
2. Tap "Keypad" at the bottom of your screen.
3. Dial the number you want to call.
4. Tap the green call button to initiate the call.
5. If you make a mistake while dialing, tap the "Delete" button to erase any errors.
6. To save the phone number to your contacts, tap "Add Number" below the dialed number.
7. When you're done with the call, tap the red "End" button .

ADDING CONTACTS TO FAVORITES

1. Open the Phone app and go to "Favorites" at the bottom left.
2. Tap the button at the top right to access your contact list.
3. Select the contact you want to add to your favorites.
4. Choose whether you want to add a shortcut for a message, an audio call, or a video call.
5. Your favorite contacts will be listed in the "Favorites" section for quick access in the Phone app.

REDIALING AND VIEWING CALL LOGS

1. To redial a contact or the last dialed number, open the Phone app .
2. Tap "Recent" at the bottom.
3. Select the number you want to redial from your call log.
4. You can also view call details like duration by tapping the info button next to a contact or number.
5. To edit your call log or clear it entirely, tap "Edit" at the top-right corner.

RECEIVING CALLS

1. When you receive an incoming call on your locked iPhone, slide the answer button

96

to answer the call.

2. Press the side button or the volume up/down buttons to silence the call.

3. To decline the call, press the side button twice while the phone is locked.

4. If your phone is unlocked, incoming calls will either appear on the call screen or as a banner depending on your activity.

5. Use the on-screen options  or to accept, decline, send a message, or set a callback reminder.

6. During a call, you can mute your microphone, switch audio output, add more calls, or transition to FaceTime.

While on the call, you can use different controls to do the following:

Tap "Mute" to turn your mic off during the call. Your caller won't be able to hear your voice.

Tap "speaker," to choose how you want to hear your call i.e. from an earpiece, speaker, or any other Bluetooth accessories connected to your phone.

Tap "add call" and then dial any number to make a conference call **is a** or tap "FaceTime" to convert your audio call into FaceTime audio or video call

Tap "contacts" to add a person from your contacts in a conference call.

SET UP OR CHECK YOUR VOICEMAILS

Open the Phone app and tap "Voicemail" from the bar at the bottom. You'll be asked to set up your "Voicemail" the first time you open the voicemail section. Follow the instructions to set up your voicemail and password.

After finishing the setup, your voicemail will appear in the Phone app under "Voicemail." To listen to your voicemail, go to the Phone app and tap "Voicemail," tap ▶ to play your voicemail, or tap ⬆ or 🗑 to share or delete any of your voicemail messages.

PHOTOS

The Photos app 🌸 is your go-to place for organizing and managing all your cherished photos and videos. It offers a user-friendly interface to help you effortlessly view, share, and edit your visual memories. Here's a guide on how to navigate the app and make the most of your photos and videos:

VIEWING YOUR PHOTOS &

VIDEOS

1. Open the Photos app 🌸 on your device.
2. The app categorizes your media into various sections, making it easy to locate specific content. To access these sections, use the navigation bar located at the bottom of your screen.

Tap to navigate Photos.

The sections include:

Library: This section organizes your photos by days, months, and years. Tap "All Photos" to view your entire photo collection.

For You: Here, you'll find featured photos from your library, as well as those shared with you via iCloud and iMessage. It also suggests sharing options with friends and family members via iCloud.

Albums: View and organize your photos and videos into various albums. You can create new albums by tapping the ╋ icon.

Search: Use the search bar to find photos by keywords, such as places, people, dates, or any other relevant information.

By tapping on these sections in the navigation bar, you can easily switch between them to find and view your photos and videos.

•   To zoom in on a photo, use the standard pinch-to-zoom gesture by placing two fingers on the screen and spreading them apart.

•   Swipe left or right to browse through your photos and videos in full-screen mode.

•   Tap on a photo to reveal additional options, such as sharing, editing, favoriting, or deleting it.

•   In the Albums section, you can create custom albums to organize your media based on themes, events, or people.

•   The Search feature is handy for quickly finding specific photos or videos by entering keywords like "beach," "birthday," or a person's name.

Tap a circle to name someone identified in the photo.

Swipe to browse through your photos.

Tap to navigate Photos.

VIEWING AND EDITING PHOTOS

•   To view an individual photo, simply tap on it. You can zoom in and out using the pinch-to-zoom gesture or double-tap.

•   Use the sliding bar 〈 at the bottom of the screen to slide between other photos.

- Tap "Edit" to access editing options. Here, you can apply filters, adjust colors, and make various edits to enhance your photos.

ORGANIZING AND MANAGING PHOTOS

- Tap the share icon to access sharing and other options.
- You can hide a photo by tapping "Hide." It will be moved to the hidden album.
- To view hidden photos, go to albums and tap "Hidden."
- You can view additional information about a photo, such as the time it was taken, location, people in the photo, camera lens details, and file size by tapping the ⓘ icon.
- Add photos to your "Favorite" album by tapping the heart icon. To view your favorite photos, go to albums and select "Favorite."

DELETING AND RECOVERING PHOTOS

- To delete a photo, tap the trash icon 🗑. Deleted photos go to the "Recently Deleted" album.
- Photos stay in "Recently Deleted" for 30 days before being permanently removed.
- To recover deleted photos, go to "Recently Deleted," tap "Select," choose the photos to recover, and tap "Recover" or "Delete."

USING PHOTOS WITH ICLOUD

- Enable iCloud Photos in Settings [Your Name] > iCloud. This backs up, shares, and syncs your photos across all your iOS devices.
- Choose "Optimize iPhone Storage" to save space by keeping a lower-quality copy on your device while storing the original quality in iCloud.
- Alternatively, select "Download and Keep Originals" to keep the highest quality photos and videos on both your device and iCloud.
- Turn on "My Photo Stream" and "Shared Album" to share and stream photos with other iOS devices and people. Access shared albums and streamed photos in the "Albums" section of the Photos app.

By following these steps, you can efficiently manage and enjoy your photo collection using the Photos app, whether it's for personal use or sharing with friends and family.

PODCAST

Explore a wide range of podcasts across various categories using the Apple Podcast app . This app allows you to subscribe to audio shows, download fresh episodes, and enjoy them while on the move.

FINDING AND FOLLOWING PODCASTS

1. Open the Podcast app and tap "Browse" at the bottom of your screen to see trending and top-charting shows.
2. To explore podcasts in specific categories like sports, science, technology, or others, tap the "Search" button at the bottom of your screen.
3. Browse the categories and tap on a show that interests you.
4. To follow a show, tap the ⊕ button.

MANAGING YOUR PODCAST SUBSCRIPTIONS

1. To control notifications, downloads, and other options for a specific podcast, tap the show, and then tap the three dots icon ••• next to the show's name.
2. You can enable automatic downloads for the show by tapping "Settings" and turning on "Automatic Download."
3. To manage notifications for all the shows you follow, tap your profile icon 👤 in the upper-left corner of the Podcast app and then tap "Notifications." Here, you can toggle notifications on or off for individual shows.

LISTENING AND ORGANIZING YOUR PODCASTS

1. Tap "Library" to access and organize your followed shows.
2. Within the Library section, you'll find the following categories:

   • "Shows": Lists all the podcast shows you follow.

   • "Saved"  : Contains episodes you've saved from different shows.

   • "Downloaded": Keeps downloaded episodes for offline listening.

   • "Latest Episodes": Shows the newest episodes from your followed shows.

   • "Listen Now": Displays podcasts you were listening to previously and recently played episodes from all your shows.

CONTROLLING YOUR PODCAST PLAYBACK

1. While listening to a podcast, use the playback controls:

   • Tap the play/pause button to control playback.

   • Swipe left or right to rewind or fast-forward.

   • Adjust the volume and playback speed as needed.

   • Use connected Bluetooth devices for playback.
2. Tap the three dots icon ••• to access additional options, such as downloading episodes or adding them to your queue.

With these steps, you can easily discover, follow, and enjoy podcasts on your Apple Podcast app, making it a seamless experience for your audio entertainment.

REMINDERS

Use the Reminder app to effectively manage your tasks and to-do lists, ensuring productivity and attentiveness to your priorities. This app allows you to create reminders with specific times, locations, or attachments to enhance your task management.

CREATING REMINDERS

1. Open the Reminder app and tap "Add List" to initiate a new list of reminders, such as "Work" or "Grocery," and begin adding tasks or to-do items.
2. Within your newly created list, tap "New Reminder" to add individual reminders.

Alternatively, you can directly create a new reminder by tapping "New Reminder" at the bottom-left corner of the Reminder app screen.

WHEN CREATING A NEW REMINDER, FOLLOW THESE STEPS

- Tap the icon to set a date and time for your reminder.
- Use the location icon to specify a location for your reminder to trigger alerts when you enter the designated area.
- Flag important reminders with the flag icon for easy identification.
- Add tags to your reminder by tapping "#."
- Include photos from your library or capture new ones by tapping . You can also scan and attach important documents.

COMPLETING, MODIFYING, OR DELETING/MANAGING YOUR REMINDERS

To make updates or edit the timing of your reminders, follow these steps:
1. Tap the specific reminder in your list.
2. Tap the pencil icon to access editing options.

Here's what you can do:

- Add URLs and notes to provide additional information.
- Include subtasks to break down complex tasks into manageable steps.

104

- Assign priorities, choosing from high, medium, or low to aid in task organization, especially when dealing with lengthy lists.

- Use the "List" option to transfer the reminder from one list to another.

You can also make adjustments to other details like the reminder's time, date, or location by tapping ⓘ.

To mark a task as complete, return to your reminder list and tap the empty circle next to the reminder. It will change to blue, signifying that the task has been accomplished. Completed reminders are automatically hidden from your list. To reveal all completed tasks, tap the ellipsis icon ⋯ at the top-right corner of the screen and select "Show Completed." To remove all completed tasks, tap "Clear."

If you want to delete reminders, go to your reminder list, swipe left on the reminder you want to remove, and then tap the "Delete" button to erase it from the list.

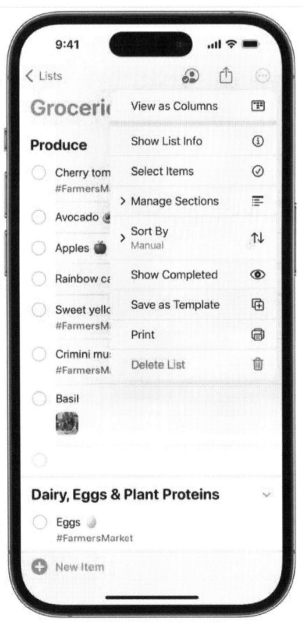

SAFARI

In the Safari app 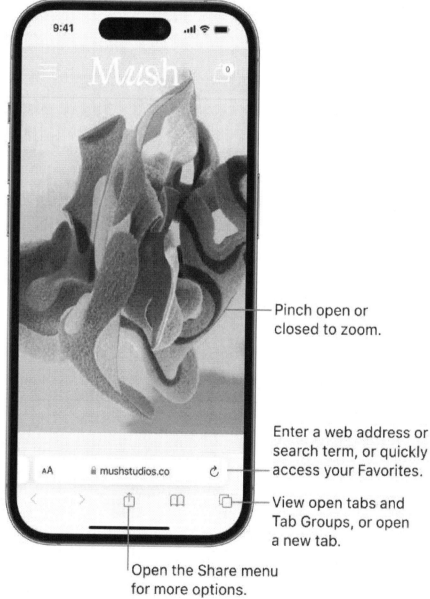, you are presented with a versatile and user-friendly web browsing experience that empowers you to explore websites, preview links, translate webpages, and recover the Safari app if, by chance, it vanishes from your Home Screen. Additionally, by syncing your Apple ID across multiple devices through iCloud, you can effortlessly maintain synchronization of your open tabs, bookmarks, history, and Reading List across all your gadgets.

VIEWING WEBSITES

• To get to a specific webpage, simply enter the website's address or search query into the address bar.

• Returning to the top of a lengthy page can be swiftly achieved with a double-tap on the top edge of the screen.

• Expand your view by simply rotating your iPhone to landscape orientation.

• When it comes to refreshing a page, a downward pull from the page's top accomplishes the task.

• Sharing links with others is made simple by tapping the Share button located at the page's bottom.

Pinch open or closed to zoom.

Enter a web address or search term, or quickly access your Favorites.

View open tabs and Tab Groups, or open a new tab.

Open the Share menu for more options.

PREVIEWING WEBSITE LINKS

• Should you wish to preview a link without fully opening the page, a touch and hold action on the link is all that's needed.

- To open the link, proceed to tap the preview, or select "Open."

- To exit the preview mode and stay on your current page, tapping anywhere outside the preview region suffices.

TRANSLATING WEBPAGES OR IMAGES

- If you ever encounter a webpage or image in a foreign language, Safari can step in to translate the text (please note that translation availability may vary based on language and region).

- Tap the Page Settings button AA, then tap the Translate button (if translation is available).

ADDING SAFARI BACK TO YOUR HOME SCREEN

- In the event that Safari mysteriously disappears from your Home Screen, fret not, for you can retrieve it from the App Library and restore it to its rightful place.

- Swipe left on your Home Screen until you reach the App Library.

- In the search field, type "Safari."

- Locate the Safari app icon, press and hold it, then choose "Add to Home Screen."

SEARCHING THE WEB

1. Launch the Safari app.
2. In the search field at the top of the screen, input your search term, phrase, or website URL.
3. You can either tap on one of the suggested search terms or simply tap "Go" on the keyboard to initiate the search.

ACCESSING YOUR FAVORITE WEBSITES WHILE SEARCHING

1. Navigate to Settings > Safari > Favorites.
2. Select the folder containing your favorite websites.
3. Now, when you begin a search in Safari, you can conveniently access your favorite websites from there.

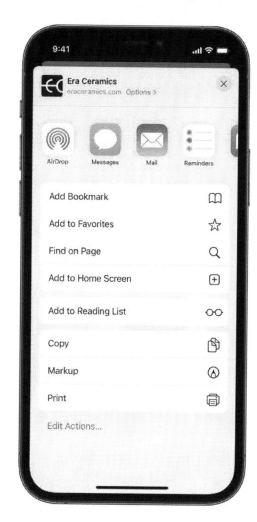

Add Bookmark or Favorite a link to save & quickly access them quickly from your Safari start page.

Tap "Find on Page" to search any keyword on a webpage.

To add webpage shortcut directly to your home screen, tap "Add to Home Screen". The link will appear on your home screen, place it anywhere with your apps for quick access.

Create your own reading list to add web pages. You can see your reading list on the Safari start page.

SEARCHING WITHIN A WEBPAGE

1. While viewing a webpage, tap the Share button ⬆️ .From the options that appear, tap "Find on Page."
2. Enter the word or phrase you're looking for in the search field.
3. To navigate to other instances of the word or phrase on the webpage, tap the ⌄ button.

CHOOSING A SEARCH ENGINE

Customize your default search engine by navigating to Settings 🌐 > Safari > Search Engine. There, you can select your preferred search engine from the available options.

OPENING A LINK IN A NEW TAB

1. To open a link in a new tab, tap and hold on the link.
2. Subsequently, tap "Open in New Tab."

   • If your prefer to remain on your current webpage when opening new links in a separate tab, open Settings 🌐 > Safari > Open Links, and then select "In Background."`

VIEWING A TAB'S HISTORY

You can conveniently review the webpages you've previously visited within a tab by performing a touch and hold action on either the Back button or the Forward button.

CLOSING TABS

To close a specific tab, execute the following steps:
1. Tap the Tabs button .
2. Tap the Close button ⊗ in the upper-right corner of that tab.

To close all tabs within a Tab Group, complete the following steps:
1. Touch and hold "Done" located at the bottom of the screen.
2. Then, tap "Close All Tabs."

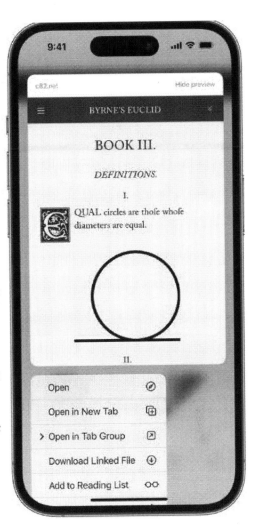

REOPENING A RECENTLY CLOSED TAB

1. Tap the Tabs button .
2. Proceed to touch and hold the New Tab button ╋.
3. From the list of recently closed tabs that emerges, select one to reopen.

PRIVATE BROWSING

1. Open the Safari app on your iPhone.
2. Tap the Tabs button .
3. Swipe right on the tab bar at the bottom of the screen until you reach Private Browsing, then tap "Unlock."

EXITING PRIVATE BROWSING

To exit Private Browsing, tap the Tabs button , then swipe left to open a Tab Group from the menu at the bottom of your screen.

STOCKS

The Stocks app on your iPhone is a powerful tool that allows you to keep a close eye on market activities, add companies to your watchlist, and access essential statistics, charts, and news at your fingertips. Let's explore how to effectively use the Stocks app to stay informed about the financial world.

ADDING OR REMOVING COMPANIES FROM YOUR WATCHLIST

Your watchlist is your personalized dashboard for tracking stock prices, percentage changes, and market values. To add or remove companies, funds, or indices from your watchlist, follow these steps:

1. Open the Stocks app and navigate to the search bar.
2. Enter the name, symbol, fund, or index of the company you want to track and tap "Search."
3. From the search results, tap your desired stock, and then tap either + or ≔, add to watch list.

TO REMOVE A COMPANY OR STOCK FROM YOUR WATCHLIST

1. Open the Stocks app and access your watchlist.
2. Swipe the stock to the left of your screen, then tap the trash icon to remove it.

Alternatively:

1. Go to your watchlist in the Stocks app.
2. Tap "Edit" in the top right corner.
3. Tap and hold the icon next to the stock you want to remove.
4. Drag the stock to a new position or tap "Remove" to delete it.

REARRANGE YOUR WATCHLIST

To customize the order of stocks in your watchlist:

1. Tap at the top of your watchlist.
2. Select "Edit."
3. Tap and hold the on next to a stock, then move it to the desired position.

VIEWING STOCK ACTIVITY FROM YOUR WATCHLIST

Once you've added stocks to your watchlist, you can access detailed data and charts about their performance. Here's how:

1. Open your watchlist in the Stocks app .
2. Tap the stock you want to explore to access charts, performance metrics, and news.

INTERACTING WITH STOCK CHARTS

The Stocks app provides interactive charts that illustrate how a stock is performing over time. To get more information from the charts, do the following:

- To see the stock's performance at a specific time, tap and hold the chart with one finger at that point.

- To view the stock's value at a particular time, tap and hold the chart with two fingers at that point.

- To access additional data like highs, lows, Beta, and EPS, swipe down on the information displayed just below the charts.

READING NEWS STORIES ABOUT YOUR STOCKS

The Stocks app integrates seamlessly with Apple News to deliver news related to the companies on your watchlist. You can access stories about a company's activities and recent events, which can help you gain insights into market trends. Here's how to access news stories about your stocks:

1. Open your watchlist in the Stocks app .
2. Tap the stock you're interested in.
3. Scroll to the bottom of the stock's page, and you'll find all the news stories related to that company or stock.

TIPS

UNLOCK THE POWER OF YOUR IPHONE

The Tips app 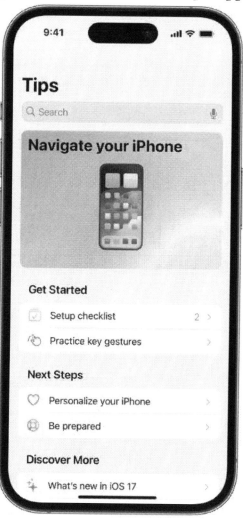 on your iPhone is your personal guide to unlocking its full potential. It provides a wealth of tips, tricks, and shortcuts to help you navigate your device more efficiently and make the most out of its features.

ORGANIZED TIPS AND GESTURES

The Tips app categorizes its content into different categories, making it easy to find information on specific apps or gestures. Simply tap on a category to explore various tips and instructions.

STAY UP-TO-DATE

The Tips app is regularly updated with new tips and features, ensuring you stay current with the latest iPhone capabilities.

GET NOTIFIED

To receive notifications whenever a new tip is available, follow these steps:
1. 1. Open Settings on your iPhone.
2. 2. Scroll down and tap "Notifications."
3. 3. Find and select "Tips" from the list of apps.
4. 4. Choose your preferred notification settings to receive alerts about new tips.

TRANSLATE

Your iPhone comes equipped with the Translate app, a versatile tool that allows you to translate text, voice, and even have conversations in various supported languages. You can also download languages for offline translation, making it a handy companion for international travel or communicating with people from different linguistic backgrounds.

TRANSLATING TEXT OR VOICE

To translate text or your voice using the Translate app, follow these steps:

1. Open the Translate app  on your iPhone.
2. Select the language you want to translate your text or voice into.
3. To swap the source and target languages, tap the button.
4. Choose one of the following options:

   • To translate text, tap "Enter text," type your phrase (or paste text), and then tap "Next" on the keyboard.

   • To translate your voice, tap the button, and then speak your phrase.

5. As you type or speak, the app will provide real-time translations.
6. After the translation is displayed, you can:

   • Play the audio translation by tapping the Play button.

   • Show the translation in full screen by tapping Enter Full Screen .

   • Save the translation as a favorite using the "Favorite" button.

   • Copy the translation to your clipboard by tapping the Copy button .

TRANSLATING CONVERSATIONS

The Translate app 🔲 also allows you to have conversations in different languages. Here's how:

1. Tap the "Conversation" tab.
2. Choose either:

   • Type text: Tap "Enter text," type your message (or paste text), and then tap "Done."

   • Use your voice: Tap the 🎤 button and speak your message.

3. Tap Play ▶ to hear the audio translation. to automate audo translations, tap ⋯, then tap Play Translations.
4. When having face-to-face conversations, tap "View" in the top left corner, then select "Face to Face" so that each person can see the conversation from their perspective.

CHOOSING MEANINGS AND GENDER VARIATIONS

When translating a word with multiple meanings or gender variations, you can select the intended meaning or gender. Here's how:

1. Open the Translate app 🔲 on your iPhone.
2. Translate a word or phrase, then tap "Next" on the keyboard.
3. When available, you can:

   • Choose a different meaning by tapping the light-colored word.

   • Select feminine or masculine translations for words with gender variations.

4. To disable grammatical gender translations, tap the ⋯ button, then tap "Show Grammatical Gender."

DOWNLOADING LANGUAGES FOR OFFLINE TRANSLATION

You can download languages to use for offline translation or when On-Device Mode is active. To download languages, follow these steps:

1. Go to Settings ⚙ > "Translate" on your iPhone.
2. In "Downloaded Languages," tap the ⬇ button next to the languages you want to install.

TRANSLATING TEXT IN APPS

Your iPhone allows you to translate text in various apps, including Camera, Photos, Safari, Messages, Mail, and supported third-party apps. Here's how:

1. Select the text you want to translate within the app.
2. Tap "Translate."
3. If you don't see Translate tap the ❭ button to reveal more options.
4. Choose the target language for your translation.
5. Below the translation, you can:

   - Replace the original text with the translation (if the text is editable).

   - Copy the translated text.

   - Add the translation to your favorites.

   - Open the translation in the Translate app.

   - Download languages for offline translation.

   - Listen to the original or translated text by tapping more, then tap ▶. To listen tap

TRANSLATING TEXT IN PHOTOS

If you have a supported model, you can translate text within photos. Here's how:
1. While viewing a photo containing text, tap the 🔲 button, then tap "Translate."
2. If you don't see "Translate," tap the ❭ button to reveal more options.

TRANSLATING TEXT WITH THE CAMERA APP

On supported models, you can use the Camera app to translate text in real time. Here's how:
1. Open the Camera app 📷 and position your iPhone to capture the text you want to translate.
2. When the yellow frame appears around detected text, tap the 🔲 button.
3. Select the text you want to translate, then tap "Translate."

   - If you don't see "Translate," tap the ❭ button for additional options.

TRANSLATING TEXT WITH THE CAMERA VIEW IN THE TRANSLATE APP

You can use the camera view in the Translate app to translate text around you, such as restaurant menus or street signs. Here's how:

1. Open the Translate app on your iPhone, then tap "Camera."
2. Choose the language you want to translate text into.
3. Position your iPhone's rear camera to view the text you want to translate.

- As you move the rear camera, the app will translate text in real time.
4. Tap the ○ button to pause the view.

   - You can zoom in to get a closer look at the overlaid translations.
5. Tap an overlaid translation to show more options, including copying or adding it to your favorites.

TRANSLATING TEXT IN PHOTOS FROM YOUR PHOTO LIBRARY

You can also translate text within photos from your photo library. Here's how:

1. Open the Translate app on your iPhone, then tap "Camera."
2. Choose the language for your translation.
3. Tap the 🖼 button, then select a photo containing text from your library.

SHARING AND SAVING TRANSLATED TEXT

After translating text from the camera view or a photo, you can share or save it in various ways. Here's how:

1. Tap the 🔼 button after translating.
2. Choose from options like sharing the translation, saving it as an image, and more.

APPLE TV

Connecting Apps and Adding Your TV Provider to the Apple TV App on Your iPhone

The Apple TV app  offers a wide range of shows and movies from streaming services and cable and satellite providers, all in one convenient place. You can access the Apple TV app on your iPhone, iPad, Mac, Apple TV, and supported smart TVs and streaming devices, ensuring you can enjoy your favorite content at home or on the go.

CONNECTING VIDEO STREAMING APPS

The Apple TV app can recommend new content or the next episode in a series from connected streaming apps. To connect supported streaming apps, follow these steps:

1. Tap "Watch Now" and scroll down to the "Streaming Apps" row.
2. Choose a streaming app from the list.
3. If the app you want to connect isn't listed, swipe left and tap "Connect More Streaming Apps."
4. Follow the onscreen instructions to connect the app.

To disconnect supported streaming apps, tap your picture or initials in the top left corner, then tap "Connected Apps."

ADDING YOUR CABLE OR SATELLITE SERVICE

With single sign-on, you can gain immediate access to all the supported video apps in your cable or satellite subscription package. Here's how:

1. Go to Settings > "TV Provider" on your iPhone.
2. Select your TV provider and sign in with your provider credentials.
If your TV provider isn't listed, you can sign in directly from the app you wish to use.

117

SUBSCRIBING TO APPLE TV+, MLS SEASON PASS, AND APPLE TV CHANNELS:

In the Apple TV app , you have the option to subscribe to various services, including:

APPLE TV+: This subscription streaming service features Apple Originals, including award-winning series, documentaries, kids' entertainment, and more. New content is added regularly.

To Subscribe to Apple TV+

- Tap "Originals," then tap the subscription button.

- Review the free trial (if eligible) and subscription details, then follow the onscreen instructions.

Apple TV Channels

These allow you to subscribe to specific channels, such as Paramount+ and STARZ, without needing to download separate apps.

To Subscribe to Apple TV Channels

- Tap "Watch Now," scroll down to the "Channels" row, and tap a channel.

- Tap the subscription button, review the free trial (if eligible) and subscription details, then follow the onscreen instructions.

MANAGING SUBSCRIPTIONS AND SHARING

You can easily change or cancel your subscriptions to Apple TV+, MLS Season Pass, or Apple TV Channels. Here's how:

1. Tap "Watch Now," then tap your profile on the top right.
2. Tap "Manage Subscriptions," and follow the onscreen instructions to make changes or cancel a subscription.

Additionally, if you use Family Sharing, you can share your subscriptions with up to five other family members. Your family members can access shared subscriptions by opening the Apple TV app after your subscription begins.

DISCOVER SHOWS AND MOVIES

- Tap "Watch Now" to get personalized recommendations based on your channel subscriptions, supported apps, purchases, and viewing interests.

- Browse Apple TV Channels: Scroll down to explore the channels you subscribe to, or tap a channel to view its titles.

- See Content Shared in Messages: In the "Shared with You" row, find movies, shows, and episodes sent by friends in Messages.

- Use the Up Next Queue: This row contains titles you recently added, rented, or purchased. You can also continue watching series or movies from where you left off.

- Explore Apple TV+: Under "Originals," you'll find Apple Originals, including a variety of series, documentaries, and more. The "Up Next on Apple TV+" row keeps track of your progress in series and lets you continue watching.

- Search for Content: Tap "Search" to look for specific shows, movies, sports, and more using keywords like titles, sports, teams, cast members, Apple TV channels, or topics.

- Stream or Download Content: You can stream content from Apple TV+ and Apple TV channels directly within the Apple TV app tv. For content from other providers, you'll be directed to their respective apps. You can also download content for offline viewing by pressing ⬇ where ever you can see this icon.

- Buy, Rent, or Pre-order: In the "Store" section, you can buy or rent movies and TV shows, or pre-order items that are not yet released.

CONTROLLING PLAYBACK

While watching content in the Apple TV app, you can use playback controls to play, pause, skip forward or backward, and more. Additionally, if you use SharePlay while watching content with friends on FaceTime, these controls are shared among all participants.

MANAGING YOUR LIBRARY

Your library in the Apple TV app contains shows and movies you've purchased, rented, or downloaded. Here's how to browse and manage your library:

- Browse Your Library: Tap "Library" and choose "TV Shows," "Movies," or "Genres."

- Watch a Rented Movie: Under "Library," tap "Rentals," then select the movie you want to watch.

- Share Purchases: If you use Family Sharing, you can share your purchases with family members. Simply tap "Library," then "Family Sharing," and choose a family member.

- Remove Downloaded Items: To free up space on your device, tap "Library," then "Downloaded." Swipe left on the item you want to remove and tap "Delete."

CHANGING APPLE TV APP SETTINGS

You can adjust various settings for the Apple TV app, including streaming and download options and how the app uses your viewing history to provide recommendations. Here's how:

1. Go to Settings 🌐 > "TV."
2. Choose your preferences for streaming and download options, including settings related to the use of cellular data and Wi-Fi quality.

▶ Play: Tap the Play button to start playback.

⏸ Pause: Tap the Pause button to pause playback.

⟲ Skip 10 Seconds Backward: Tap this button to go back 10 seconds; touch and hold to rewind.

⟳ Skip 10 Seconds Forward: Tap this button to jump forward 10 seconds; touch and hold to fast-forward.

⃤ AirPlay: Use this button to stream the video to other compatible devices.

⋯ More Controls: Access additional options such as changing playback speed, enabling subtitles and closed captions, altering the language, and more.

⧉ Picture in Picture: Start Picture in Picture mode to continue watching content while using other apps.

VOICE MEMO

Capturing and Managing Audio with the Voice Memo App

With the Voice Memo app  on your iPhone, you have a versatile audio recorder at your fingertips. Whether it's taking quick voice notes, recording music practices, or saving important memos, this app has you covered. You can even back up your recordings to iCloud for added peace of mind.

RECORDING MADE EASY

To start recording, open the Voice Memo app and tap the ⚪ button. The recording will begin immediately, and you'll see the elapsed time displayed.

To stop the recording, simply tap the ⚫ button. If you'd like to mute the start and stop tones on your recording, use the volume buttons on your iPhone. Lower the volume using the volume down button, or mute it completely by going all the way down.

For more control over your recordings, you can pause ❚❚ and resume ▶.To review your recording before saving it, tap ❚❚, then ▶ when you're ready to continue. To save the recording, tap "Done".

A Voice Memo recording in progress

BACKGROUND RECORDING

Voice Memo continues recording in the background while you use other apps, making it convenient to multitask without interruption.

ENABLING ICLOUD BACKUP

To ensure your voice memos are securely backed up, follow these steps:
1. Open Settings ⚙ on your iPhone, Tap "Your Name.", Scroll down and tap "Voice Memo.", Turn on the "Voice Memo" toggle switch.

PLAYBACK AND ORGANIZATION

All your saved recordings are neatly organized in the Voice Memo app. To play a recording, simply tap on it. You can use the playback controls to play, pause, rewind, or skip forward.

For more advanced playback options, such as controlling playback speed or skipping silence, tap the "More" button and explore these features. Enhance your recordings by reducing background noise and echoes with the provided option.

ADJUSTING PLAYBACK SPEED FOR RECORDINGS

You have the option to change the playback speed of a recording, either making it faster or slower. Here's how:

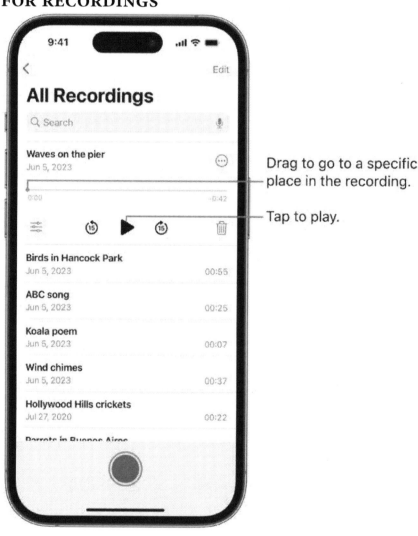

Drag to go to a specific place in the recording.

Tap to play.

2. In the list of recordings, select the one you wish to play. Tap the ⚏ button.

3. Adjust the playback speed by dragging the slider towards the tortoise 🐢 or slower speed or towards the rabbit 🐇 for faster speed.

4. Close the settings by tapping the ❌ button.

5. Finally, tap the ▶ button to start playing the recording at your chosen speed.

Note: If you wish to turn off all your playback options, tap ⚏ More, then choose "Reset."

FAVORITES AND FOLDERS

You can organize your recordings by adding them to favorites or creating folders for easy access. Rename your recordings to make them easier to identify. To add recordings to your favorites, tap ⋯, then tap the ♡ button.

To create folders and move recordings, tap ⊟⊕ on the top-right corner of your recording list. You can delete entire folders, reorder them, or create new ones as needed. To see all your folders, tap the ‹ button and tap a folder.

EDITING AND DELETING RECORDINGS

You have the flexibility to edit, re-record, or delete recordings. To trim a recording, tap the recording, then tap "Edit Recording" and use the trimming feature.

To delete a recording, tap ‹ to go back to all folders, select your folder and recording then tap ⊖ recording, then tap 🗑. For multiple deletions, enter "Edit" mode and select the recordings you want to delete.

Remember, deleted recordings are moved to "Recently Deleted" and remain there for 30 days before being permanently removed.

Control	Description
▶	Play
‖	Pause
(15)	Skip backward 15 seconds
(15)	Skip forward 15 seconds

WALLET

The Wallet app  on your iPhone is a versatile tool for managing various cards, IDs, passes, and more. It streamlines your digital life by allowing you to access these items quickly and securely. In this chapter, we'll explore how to make the most of your Wallet app.

SAVING CREDIT & DEBIT CARDS

1. Open the Wallet app .
2. Tap the ⊕ icon and follow the on-screen instructions.
3. You can add cards by taking a photo or entering the card details manually.

SETTING DEFAULT PAYMENT METHOD

Your first card will be your default payment method. To change it, tap and drag the card to the front of the stack in your Wallet app .

USING APPLE PAY FOR PAYMENTS

1. Double-press the side button to activate Apple Pay.
2. Authenticate with Face ID or your passcode.
3. Hold your iPhone near the contactless POS machine.
4. Wait until you see "Done" on your screen.

You can use Apple Pay at locations displaying the contactless payment symbols.

ONLINE SHOPPING WITH APPLE PAY

1. Choose "Apple Pay" at the checkout.
2. Confirm billing details, shipping address, and contact information.
3. Double-press the side button and authenticate the payment with Face ID or your passcode.

APPLE CASH

When you send or receive money via Messages, it seamlessly flows into your Apple Cash account within the Wallet app. You can utilize these funds for purchases at locations that accept Apple Pay or effortlessly transfer them to your bank account.

ENABLING APPLE CASH

1. Go to Settings 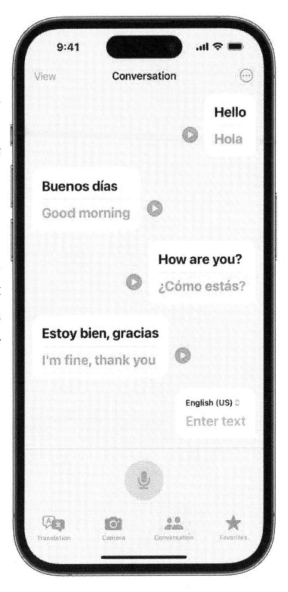 > "Wallet & Apple Pay."
2. Turn on "Apple Cash."

MANAGING APPLE CASH

1. Open the Wallet app ▭.
2. Tap "Apple Cash" to view transactions and manage your account.

ADDING YOUR APPLE CARD

1. Tap the ⊕ icon and select "Apply for Apple Card."
2. Provide required information and agree to terms.
3. Review and choose an Apple Card offer.

VIEWING APPLE CARD INFORMATION

• To view your Apple Card number, expiration date, and CVV, tap the ▭₁₂₃ icon or your card in your Wallet app

SENDING PAYMENTS WITH APPLE CASH

With Apple Cash, you can effortlessly send payments, whether it's a one-time transaction or a recurring payment that recurs weekly, bi-weekly, or monthly. Here's how:

1. Launch the Wallet app  on your iPhone.
2. Tap on your Apple Cash card, and then select "Send" or "Request."
3. Either enter the recipient's information or choose a contact from your recent list and type the payment amount.
4. Depending on your preference, choose one of the following options:

   • For a one-time payment, simply tap "Send."

   • If you wish to set up recurring payments, tap "Send Recurring Payment." Set the start date and specify the frequency of the payments. You also have the option to add a memo and choose an icon for the transaction (optional).

5. Add a comment if you want, then tap the Send button.

6. Review the information, then authenticate with Face ID, Touch ID, or your passcode.

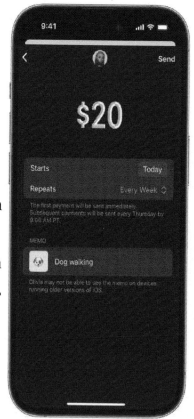

MANAGING APPLE CARD

TRANSACTIONS

1. Open the Wallet app.
2. Tap your "Apple Card" to review transactions and statements.
3. Search for specific transactions or get weekly, monthly, or yearly statements.

ADDING DIGITAL KEYS

Your iPhone comes with Near Field Communication (NFC) technology to securely store digital keys, readily accessible whenever you require them. You can conveniently add keys for your car, home, or hotel to your phone, ensuring easy access while minimizing the risk of losing them unexpectedly.

NFC technology detects your proximity to your car, home lock, or hotel room, automatically displaying your keycard on the lock screen for swift access. Simply hold the top of your iPhone near your car, home, or hotel lock, and it will effortlessly unlock. Additionally, you can access your keycard through your Apple Watch.

For Cars and Hotels:

In the case of cars and hotel rooms, you may need to download the respective apps provided by the car manufacturer and your hotel. To add keys to your home, use the Apple Home app to access them within your Wallet app.

APPLE CARD - YOUR DIGITAL CREDIT COMPANION

Apple Card is Apple's innovative credit card, designed to simplify your financial life while offering clear and transparent financial management. You can easily apply for and use Apple Card on your iPhone, enhancing your purchasing power both in-store and online.

GETTING YOUR APPLE CARD

1. Open the Wallet app on your iPhone.
2. Tap the button and select "Apply for Apple Card."
3. Complete the necessary information and agree to the terms and conditions.
4. Review your Apple Card offer, including the credit limit and APR, and decide whether to accept or decline the offer.

If you accept, you can also set Apple Card as your default payment method for Apple Pay transactions and order a physical titanium Apple Card for places where Apple Pay isn't accepted.

USING APPLE CARD

You can use Apple Card wherever Apple Pay is accepted, including:

- Making contactless payments using Apple Pay.

- Paying in apps or on the web with Apple Pay.

- For locations where Apple Pay isn't available, you can access your card details:

- In apps, online, or over the phone: Tap the   button in Wallet to reveal your card number, expiration date, and security code.

- In physical stores, restaurants, and other places: Use the titanium Apple Card.

MANAGING TRANSACTIONS AND STATEMENTS

- Open Wallet and tap Apple Card then tap .
- Review your transactions, which are grouped by month and year.
- Search your transactions using 🔍 & keywords, categories, merchants, or locations.
- Analyze your spending by viewing weekly, monthly, or yearly activity, and swipe right to see previous periods.
- Access your monthly statements, including a summary, PDF statement, and transaction export options.

MAKING PAYMENTS

- In Wallet , tap "Apple Card."
- Tap the payment button and choose one of the following options:
- Pay immediately: Set the amount, drag the checkmark (or tap "Other Amount"), and tap "Pay."
- Schedule a one-time payment: Set the amount, schedule a date, and tap "Pay."
- Set up automatic payments: Configure recurring payments for the monthly balance, minimum balance due, or a custom amount, with the option to choose the due date.

APPLE CARD WIDGET

- Add the Apple Card widget to your Home Screen to monitor your balance, available credit, and spending activity at a glance.
- Customize the widget to display spending activity for a different time period.

TRACK YOUR ORDERS WITH IPHONE WALLET

You can keep tabs on your purchases made through participating apps and websites by tracking your orders directly in the Wallet app.

WEATHER

The Weather app ☁ on your iPhone is your go-to source for staying updated on current weather conditions and forecasts. Here's how to make the most of it:

CHECKING YOUR LOCAL WEATHER

1. Open the Weather app ☁ on your iPhone, and it will automatically display the weather report for your current location.

2. Key information you can find:

   • Hourly forecasts below the temperature. Swipe to see more hourly forecasts.

   • Swipe up to access the 10-day weather forecast.

   • View local weather on the map.

   • Check the air quality of your location.

   • Scroll down for additional details like sunset and sunrise times, wind speed and direction, and the UV Index.

ADDING AND MANAGING LOCATIONS

1. You can add multiple locations to your Weather app for quick access to weather updates from various places.
2. To add a new location, tap the "Add" button at the bottom corner of the app.
3. Enter the name of the city you want to add in the search bar and tap it when it appears in the search results.
4. Tap "Add" at the top-left corner to include it in your weather list.

TO REMOVE A CITY FROM YOUR LIST

   • Swipe left on the city name you want to remove, and then tap "Delete". Alternatively, tap the "Edit list" option at the top-right corner, and then remove the city.

TO REORDER YOUR LOCATIONS

   • Tap "Edit" in your weather list, and then drag and drop the cities to rearrange them.

CUSTOMIZING NOTIFICATIONS AND TEMPERATURE UNITS

1. In the weather list, tap the "More" button to access additional options.
2. You can choose to:

   • "Edit list" to manage locations.

   • Enable "Notification" to receive weather alerts for conditions like rain, snow, or sleet. Ensure you've allowed location access for the Weather app in your device settings to receive notifications according to your location.

   • Switch between Celsius and Fahrenheit for temperature units.

   • Use the "Report an Issue" option if you find inaccuracies in the weather information.

EXPLORING WEATHER MAPS

Weather maps provide a visual overview of weather conditions in your area and beyond. Here's how to use them:
1. Open a weather location from your list.
2. Tap the "Maps" button at the bottom-left corner.
You can:

   • Switch between different map views such as Air Quality, Precipitation, and Temperature.

   • Zoom in and out by pinching the screen or tap and hold with one finger to navigate the map.

   • Tap and hold on a location on the map to access additional options like adding it to your list or viewing its weather forecast.

   • Use the "Next" button to switch between locations from your list.
When you're done with the weather maps, simply tap "Done" at the top-left corner to return to the standard view.

UNDERSTANDING WEATHER ICONS

Here's a quick reference guide to help you interpret these icons:

  Sunrise   Sunset

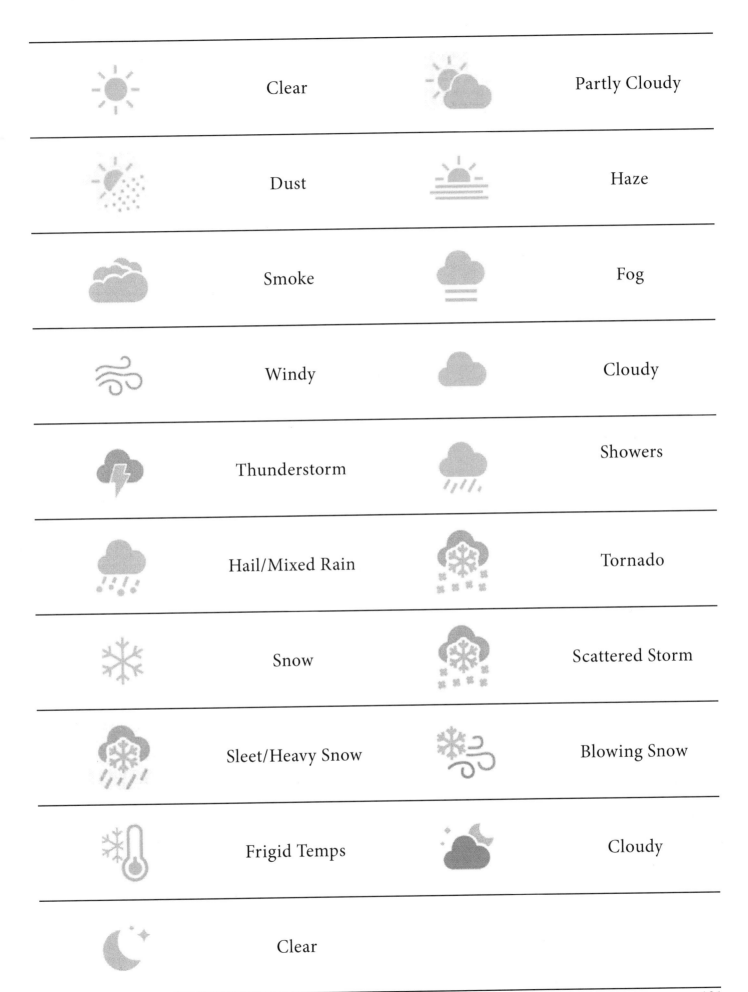

	Clear		Partly Cloudy
	Dust		Haze
	Smoke		Fog
	Windy		Cloudy
	Thunderstorm		Showers
	Hail/Mixed Rain		Tornado
	Snow		Scattered Storm
	Sleet/Heavy Snow		Blowing Snow
	Frigid Temps		Cloudy
	Clear		

Update, Backup, Restore & Reset Your iPhone

TURNING YOUR IPHONE ON AND OFF

To ensure your iPhone operates smoothly and efficiently, it's important to know how to power it on and off properly. Here are the steps:

TURNING ON YOUR IPHONE

Press and hold the side button (also known as the power button) until you see the Apple logo appear on the screen. This signifies that your iPhone is starting up.

TURNING OFF YOUR IPHONE

The method for turning off your iPhone depends on the model you have:

IPHONE WITH FACE ID

1. Simultaneously press and hold the side button (power button) and either of the volume buttons until you see a slider on the screen.
2. Drag the slider labeled "Power Off" to the right. This action will shut down your iPhone.

IPHONE WITH A HOME BUTTON

1. Press and hold the side button (power button) until you see a slider on the screen.
2. Drag the slider labeled "Power Off" to the right to turn off your iPhone.

For all iPhone models, you can also use the following method to turn off your device:
1. Go to Settings on your iPhone.

2. Scroll down and select General.

3. Scroll to the bottom of the General settings and tap Shut Down. A slider will appear; slide it to power off your iPhone.

FORCE RESTARTING YOUR IPHONE

If your iPhone becomes unresponsive and turning it off and on doesn't resolve the issue, you can try force restarting it. Here's how:

1. Quickly press and release the volume up button.

2. Quickly press and release the volume down button.

3. Press and hold the side button until you see the Apple logo appear on the screen. Release the side button at this point.

This force restart process varies slightly for older iPhone models, such as the iPhone 7, iPhone 6s, or iPhone SE (1st generation). If you're using one of these models, please refer to the iOS 15 version of the instructions.

If your iPhone still doesn't respond after trying these steps, you may need to visit the Apple Support website for further assistance.

UPDATING IOS ON YOUR IPHONE

Keeping your iPhone's operating system up to date is essential for its security and performance. Here's how to update iOS:

AUTOMATIC UPDATES

If you didn't enable automatic updates during the initial setup of your iPhone, follow these steps:

1. Open Settings on your iPhone.

2. Scroll down and select General.

3. Tap Software Update.

4. Toggle on Automatic Updates under "Automatically Install" and "Automatically Download."

With automatic updates enabled, your iPhone will download and install new iOS updates overnight while connected to Wi-Fi and charging.

MANUAL UPDATES

To manually check for and install iOS updates:

1. Open Settings on your iPhone.
2. Scroll down and select General.
3. Tap Software Update.

Here, you can check if an update is available and choose to download and install it manually.

UPDATING USING A COMPUTER

If you prefer to update iOS using your computer, follow these steps:

ON A MAC (MACOS 10.15 OR LATER)

1. Connect your iPhone to your Mac using a USB cable.
2. In the Finder sidebar, select your iPhone.
3. Click General at the top of the Finder window.
4. Click Check for Update and follow the onscreen instructions to update your iPhone.

ON A MAC (MACOS 10.14 OR EARLIER) OR A WINDOWS PC

1. Open the iTunes app (make sure you have the latest version).
2. Connect your iPhone to your computer using a USB cable.
3. Click the button that resembles an iPhone near the top-left corner of the iTunes window.
4. Click Summary and then click **Check for Update.** Follow the prompts to update your iPhone.

Remember that it's essential to keep your iPhone updated to benefit from the latest features, improvements, and security enhancements.

BACKING UP YOUR IPHONE

Regularly backing up your iPhone is crucial to safeguard your data. You can choose to back up your device using iCloud or your computer. Here's how:

BACKING UP WITH ICLOUD

1. Go to Settings on your iPhone.
2. Tap your Apple ID at the top of the screen (it may also be labeled as your name).
3. Select iCloud and then tap iCloud Backup.
4. Turn on iCloud Backup.

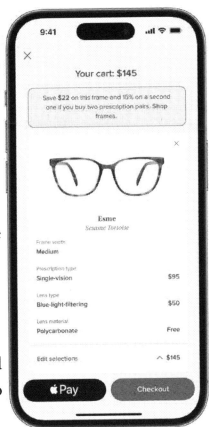

Your iPhone will automatically back up daily when connected to power, locked, and connected to Wi-Fi. You can also perform a manual backup by tapping Back Up Now.

To view your iCloud backups, navigate to Settings > [your name] > iCloud > Manage Account Storage > Backups. Here, you can delete or manage backups.

BACKING UP WITH YOUR COMPUTER

(MAC OR WINDOWS PC)

1. Connect your iPhone to your computer using a USB cable.
2. If you're using a Mac (macOS 10.15 or later), open the Finder and select your iPhone from the sidebar. Click General and check the box for Back up all of the data on your iPhone to this Mac. Optionally, you can select *Encrypt local backup* to protect it with a password. Finally, click Back Up Now.
3. If you're using an older Mac (macOS 10.14 or earlier) or a Windows PC, open iTunes, click the iPhone button near the top-left corner, select **Summary**, and click Back Up Now. Remember to update iTunes to the latest version if necessary.

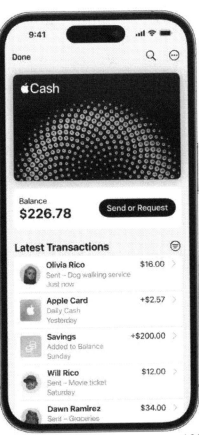

RESTORING IPHONE SETTINGS TO DEFAULTS

If you want to reset your iPhone's settings to their defaults without erasing your content, follow these steps:

1. Go to Settings ⚙ on your iPhone.
2. Scroll down and select General.
3. Tap Transfer or Reset iPhone and then choose Reset.
4. Depending on your preference, you can select from these options:

    • Reset All Settings: Resets all settings, including network settings, keyboard dictionary, location settings, privacy settings, and Apple Pay cards. No data or media are deleted.

    • Reset Network Settings: Clears all network settings, including Wi-Fi networks and VPN configurations. Also resets the device name to "iPhone" and changes manually trusted certificates to untrusted.

    • Reset Keyboard Dictionary: Removes words added to the keyboard dictionary.

    • Reset Home Screen Layout: Restores built-in apps to their original layout on the Home Screen.

    • Reset Location & Privacy: Returns location services and privacy settings to their defaults.

Choose the appropriate option, and your iPhone's settings will be reset accordingly.

Please note that if you select "Erase All Content and Settings," all data on your iPhone will be deleted.

RESTORING IPHONE FROM A BACKUP

If you need to restore your content, settings, and apps from a backup to a new or freshly erased iPhone, follow these steps:

RESTORING FROM AN ICLOUD BACKUP

1. Turn on your new or freshly erased iPhone.
2. During the setup process, you can choose Set Up Manually and then select Restore from iCloud Backup. Follow the onscreen instructions to complete the process.

Alternatively, if you have another iOS device with iOS 11, iPadOS 13, or later, you can use the Quick Start feature to transfer settings and content to your new device automatically.

For devices running iOS 12.4 or later, you can transfer data wirelessly between devices.

RESTORING FROM A COMPUTER BACKUP (MAC OR WINDOWS PC)

1. Connect your new or freshly erased iPhone to your computer using a USB cable.
2. Depending on your computer's operating system, use the Finder (macOS 10.15 or later) or iTunes (macOS 10.14 or earlier, or Windows PC) to initiate the restore process. Select the appropriate backup from the list and follow the prompts.

If your backup is encrypted, you will need to enter the encryption password to restore your data and settings.

ERASING IPHONE

If you need to permanently erase all content and settings from your iPhone, follow these instructions:

USING SETTINGS TO ERASE IPHONE

1. Go to Settings on your iPhone.
2. Scroll down and select General.
3. Tap Transfer or Reset iPhone.
4. Choose one of the following options:

   • Get Started: This option allows you to prepare your content and settings for transfer to a new iPhone. After preparing, return to Settings > General > Transfer or Reset iPhone and select Erase All Content and Settings.

   • Erase All Content and Settings: This option will completely erase all data and settings from your iPhone.

USING A COMPUTER TO ERASE IPHONE

To erase your iPhone using a computer, follow these steps:
1. Connect your iPhone to your computer with a USB cable.
2. Use the Finder (macOS 10.15 or later) or iTunes (macOS 10.14 or earlier, or Windows PC) to perform the erase process. Click Restore iPhone or a similar option, and follow the onscreen instructions.

Before erasing your iPhone, make sure to back up your data if needed, as this process will permanently remove all content and settings. Additionally, ensure you have your iPhone passcode and Apple ID password on hand.

Caution: Erasing your iPhone is irreversible, and all data will be permanently deleted. Make sure to back up your important information before proceeding.

47171878R00078